# Bullet Proof Your Co
# Limited Liability Company and Limited Partnership



## Protecting the Corporate Veil

by Garrett Sutton, Esq.

**A SuccessDNA Nonfiction Book**



**Disclaimer**

Information Only – Not Legal Advice • The information in the book is for your general use. It should not be taken as legal advice, or in the place of legal advice. This information has been prepared on the basis of general state and federal laws. Nevertheless, your local laws may have provisions in them that conflict with this information or override them completely. We have no way of telling you how the laws of your state, province or country will affect the operation of your business. You will need to seek the advice from an attorney to be sure of how this information may be used in your state.

No Attorney-Client Relationship Formed • Your use of this information does not create an attorney-client relationship between you and Sutton Law Center, P.C. The fact that you may send an email message to any member of this firm regarding this information or any other questions also does not create an attorney-client relationship.

No Specialist Certification • Although we state that our practice is limited to corporate, transactional and business issues, that does not make us "experts" or "specialists" in that field. To be considered as an expert or specialist requires a special certification by an attorney's local Bar Association. In fact, the State Bar of Nevada does not certify any lawyer as a specialist or an expert. Neither the State Bar of Nevada nor any agency of the State Bar has certified any lawyer with our firm as a specialist or as an expert. Anyone considering retaining a lawyer should independently investigate that lawyer's credentials and ability.

Second Edition: 2011

Printed in the United States of America

10 9 8 7 6 5 4 3 2 1

Library of Congress Control Number: ISBN 0-9746844-1-4 978-0-97468-441-3

Cover design by Max Good • Project X Grapics | Interior Design by PCI Publishing Group

# About the Author

Garrett Sutton, Esq., is the bestselling author of *Start Your Own Corporation, Run Your Own Corporation, The ABCs of Getting Out of Debt, Writing Winning Business Plans, Buying and Selling a Business* and *The Loopholes of Real Estate* in Robert Kiyosaki's Rich Dad Advisors series. Garrett has over thirty years experience in assisting individuals and business to determine their appropriate corporate structure, limit their liability, protect their assets and advance their financial, personal and credit success goals.

Garrett and his law firm, Sutton Law Center, have offices in Reno, Nevada, Jackson Hole, Wyoming and Sacramento, California. The firm represents many corporations, limited liability companies, limited partnerships and individuals in their real estate and business-related law matters, including incorporations, contracts, and ongoing business-related legal advice. The firm continues to accept new clients.

Garrett is also the owner of Corporate Direct, which since 1988 has provided affordable asset protection and corporate formation services. He is the author of *How to Use Limited Liability Companies and Limited Partnerships*, published by Success DNA, which further educates readers on the proper use of entities. Along with credit expert Gerri Detweiler, Garrett also assists entrepreneurs build business credit. Please see www.businesscreditsuccess.com for more information.

Garrett attended Colorado College and the University of California at Berkeley, where he received a B.S. in Business Administration in 1975. He graduated with a J.D. in 1978 from Hastings College of Law, the University of California's law school in San Francisco. He has appeared in the Wall Street Journal, The New York Times and other publications.

Garrett is a member of the State Bar of Nevada, the State Bar of California, and the American Bar Association. He has written numerous professional articles and has served on the Publication Committee of the State Bar of Nevada.

Garrett enjoys speaking with entrepreneurs and real estate investors on the advantages of forming business entities. He is a frequent lecturer for small business groups as well as the Rich Dad's Advisors series.

Garrett serves on the boards of the American Baseball Foundation, located in Birmingham, Alabama, and the Reno, Nevada-based Sierra Kids Foundation.

For more information on Garrett Sutton and Sutton Law Center, please visit his Web sites at www.sutlaw.com, www.corporatedirect.com, and www.successdna.com.

# Introduction

This special book is prepared to help you, the asset holder, business owner and entrepreneur, with an important element of your overall business protection plan: Following the corporate formalities so that your own personal assets are covered.

This publication is designed to provide you with the crucial information you need to protect the corporate veil from being pierced, or ignored, thus exposing your personal assets to satisfy the claims brought against your business.

If you have any questions or issue to discuss when reading this book, you may want to schedule a consultation with an attorney in our office. Please feel free to call toll free 1-800-700-1430 to learn if such a consultation would be of benefit.

While state laws vary and specific legal situations may require that you obtain legal counsel in your own area, it is felt that the information herein will provide you with a sufficient general knowledge to bullet proof your corporation.

# Table of Contents

# I. Preliminary Considerations

Whether you are just starting or have an existing business that you want to protect, you should consider the benefits a corporation may provide. If you have an ownership interest in an existing business, hopefully you are already familiar with the realities of owning your own business. If you are just beginning, you have many decisions to make before you will be ready to conduct business safely. Among the decisions you must make are whether your ideas are sufficiently developed for you to use as the basis of a business plan, whether you should rely upon investors or other forms of financing for your business, whether to form a corporation or operate your business through a different business entity, and in which state you should organize your business entity. You should only enter into business after you make these considerations and decide what is right for your situation.

This book is intended to provide a general guide for managers and Shareholders of young and developing corporations. The primary aims of this book are to discuss how to properly form a corporation and how to maintain the primary benefits of corporations: tax benefits and limited liability. The notes in the left margin provide references to resources for more information and indicate the steps necessary to raise and maintain the corporate veil.

While this book and other advisory materials may provide fundamental information that business owners need, the information provided herein does not constitute legal advice and cannot replace the services that accountants and attorneys provide. Arming yourself with knowledge may allow you to use such services more efficiently and allow your business to prosper. For more information on legal services visit www.sutlaw.com

### *Developing Your Ideas*

The first stage in the life of any business is to find and develop the perfect idea for the business. Before considering financing, forming a corporation, or entering into business, every entrepreneur must face the realities of the market and the unique characteristics of their business ideas. Advice from an attorney, accountant, or other specialist familiar with business may be valuable in deciding whether to take your idea from the drawing room to the marketplace. No matter how much capital you have or how many investors are willing to assist you, if you do not take the time to develop your ideas into a business plan and seriously consider the likelihood of success, you are not ready to begin. By developing your ideas into a business plan, you will clarify your aspirations and expectations and identify potential threats. Through careful planning, you can prevent your dreams from becoming nightmares.

*The SCORE program offered by the Small Business Administration is a free, but valuable resource in preparing and analyzing a business plan. For more information, see http://www.score.org*

### *Risks and Costs of Starting a Business*

Although you may not want to focus on the risks and costs involved in starting a business, every entrepreneur must face the risks of their business and financial realities. Statistics regarding business failure rates and the profitability of young businesses are intimidating; however, if business owners confront potential threats and engage in adequate planning, the chances of success may drastically improve. By anticipating the costs of starting a business, you will be able to avoid many common mistakes.

A common misconception about business success rates suggests that nearly ninety percent of new businesses fail within the first year. This statistic is ill conceived, because it includes entrepreneurs who do not take the time to develop their ideas or engage in necessary planning. It has been said that, if you remove obvious failures and fads, and then eliminate entrepreneurs who didn't take the time to study what they were getting into or bother themselves with drafting the dream into a coherent, well-drafted business plan, the actual success rate is closer to sixty percent. By making sure that your business idea is realistic and worthwhile, and by expending the time and energy to draft a clear business plan, you may avoid common blunders, arm yourself with tools and knowledge, and increase your chances of success.

*For information and assistance on drafting a business plan see "Writing Winning Business Plans" by Garrett Sutton.*

Another questionable observation is that, unless you have enough money to float your business for at least three full years while it remains entirely in the red, you don't have enough money to start yet. This is generally true, but may be an understatement. Each business is unique and requires its owners to carefully consider what is required for success. By mentally and financially preparing for the thin years ahead and taking steps to ensure the availability of financing, business owners can reduce the panic that often accompanies a new business. The financial obstacles can be overcome. By planning for the monetary costs and engaging in careful planning, business owners can drastically reduce the dangers involved in starting a business.

You should also consider building a business credit profile separate and apart from your personal credit. In this way you may be able to use business credit to grow your business, without being dependent on personal credit lines, which can become exhausted. It can take six months or more to build business credit, so you may want to get started right away. For more information visit www.businesscreditsuccess.com.

### *Choosing An Entity*

Although this book focuses on corporations, other entities are available that provide businesses with varying costs and benefits. After an entrepreneur thoroughly considers the risks and costs involved with taking their ideas to the marketplace, he or she should consider the benefits and drawbacks of available entities. Differences in management structure, tax liability, and financing options may guide the decision to form a corporation or use another business entity, such as a limited liability company or limited partnership. Regardless of which entity you choose, considering available options allows you to ensure that you are making an educated and reasoned decision.

Other business entities may provide some of the benefits that corporations offer. Shareholders in a corporation are not required to pay any more than what they paid for their shares. If the corporation's assets cannot satisfy the corporation's creditors, the creditors generally cannot seek satisfaction from the Shareholders' personal assets. The Shareholder's liability is limited to their initial contribution. Similarly, a limited partner or member of a limited liability company is not required to pay any more than their initial contribution or any other agreed upon contribution. Creditors cannot generally attach a limited partner's or a member's personal assets. Limited liability makes corporations, limited partnerships, limited liability limited partnerships, and limited liability companies preferable over conducting business through a partnership or sole proprietorship.

While limited liability may be provided through corporations and other entities, tax treatment and management structures allow one to differentiate between available entities. Corporations provide different tax benefits and drawbacks than do other entities, including double taxation of corporate profits and certain deductions. Differences in management structure may make one entity preferable over others. Directors and Officers manage corporations, general partner(s) manage limited partnerships and a member, members, a designated manager, or designated managers can manage limited liability companies. When deciding among business entities, an entrepreneur should consider limited liability, the entity's tax treatment, and its management structure so as to ensure that he or she selects the most appropriate entity for the business opportunity.

*For an overview of corporate management Considerations, see "Providing Management for the Corporation," below.*

### *Choosing a State*

In addition to deciding among business entities, an entrepreneur should consider the differences in states' treatment of the chosen business entity. Each state's laws affecting businesses differ slightly, and some states' laws are more favorable to business than are others. Nevada, Wyoming and Delaware are frequently chosen for their tax free, business friendly laws. Delaware is a jurisdiction of choice for forming larger corporations, because it has a wealth of court decisions defining the rights and limitations of corporations. However, Delaware has more reporting requirements than either Nevada or Wyoming. Nevada and Wyoming both allow corporations flexibility in management with fewer reporting requirements. Other states may be preferable because of the benefits they provide. An entrepreneur should consult with an accountant and an attorney to determine whether any specific jurisdiction is preferable based on its unique treatment of businesses.

*For information on entity selection, see "Start Your Own Corporation: Why the Rich Own Their Own Companies and Everyone Else Works for Them," by Garrett Sutton*

It may seem unusual to organize a business in a state other than that in which you live and work. However, the benefits of organizing your business in a different jurisdiction may be substantial. The cost of organizing in a different jurisdiction will likely be limited to the cost of retaining a resident agent in the state and paying annual fees and business taxes; however, you should consult with local legal and tax counsel to ensure that you comply with all requirements of the jurisdiction in which you form your business entity. Choosing the right state for your business could save you money and protect your business from uncertain litigation. Accordingly, every entrepreneur should consider organizing his or her business in a business friendly alternative state, such as Nevada and/or Wyoming.

# II. Forming a Corporation: Raising the Corporate Veil

Once you have decided that a corporation, LLC or LP is the right entity for your business or asset holding purpose and you have decided which state to incorporate in, corporate formalities begin. It should be noted that while some have written that corporate formalities do not apply to an LLC or LP, such a lax strategy is not good asset protection planning. While we refer to corporations in this e-book, the concepts and issues apply to LLCs and LPs as well. Don't be misled by those who would claim that the need for following formalities only applies to corporations. LLCs and LPs require (or soon will require) the easy adherence of these simple rules.

A corporation is born when the Articles of Incorporation are properly filed. Events occurring immediately after formation must be performed properly to maintain the corporate veil and ensure the corporation's longevity and flexibility.

The corporate veil provides Shareholders with limited liability and is raised and maintained by management and ownership that treats the corporation like a corporation. As indicated above, a corporation is considered to be a legally distinct entity, capable of incurring its own debts and obligations. By operating a business through a corporation or otherwise using a corporation, one may protect themselves from liability for the corporation's debts and obligations. This protection is frequently referred to as the corporate veil. When creditors or others seek to obtain a judgment from a court that makes the corporation's Shareholders, Directors, or Officers personally liable, they are seeking to pierce the corporate veil.

In seeking to pierce the corporate veil, creditors and others generally seek to show that the Shareholders, Directors or Officers failed to treat the corporation like a separate legal entity and that injustice would result if the court treated the corporation as a separate entity. To prevent creditors or others from being able to convince a court to pierce the corporate veil and disregard the corporation, the corporation must follow corporate formalities in formation and while conducting business.

## *Filing the Articles of Incorporation*

### *Step 1: Prepare and File Articles of Incorporation*

The Articles of Incorporation provide the state Secretary of State or an analogous organization with information about the corporation. When the Articles are filed along with the applicable fees, the state breathes life into the corporation by providing it with a corporate charter.

Articles of Incorporation generally provide the corporation's name, the purpose for which the corporation is formed (some states require a specific purpose, others allow the purpose of engaging in any lawful activity), the name(s) and address (es) of the initial Director(s), the total number of shares the corporation is authorized to issue, the duration of the corporation's existence (generally, perpetual), and the name and address of the corporation's reliable resident agent. Filing Articles of Incorporation necessarily involves deciding who the initial Directors(s) will be, selecting a registered agent, deciding how many and what types of shares of stock to authorize, and other issues that will guide the corporation's life. As soon as the Articles of Incorporation are filed, the corporation is a separate legal entity with rights, powers, and duties that are distinct from those of its owners and incorporator(s). Legal or other official matters pertaining to the corporation are addressed to its registered office or registered agent, which must maintain certain documents in their resident agent file. Although the corporation may exist and have a mailing address, for the corporation to begin conducting business, it must be provided with management and resources. Accordingly, the corporation's organizational meetings should be conducted

*The importance of a reliable resident agent cannot be over-stated: they provide the corporation with important notices (such as lawsuits) and are required by law in most states.*

shortly after the incorporator files the Articles of Incorporation.

## *Holding Organizational Meetings*

### *Step 2: Hold Organizational Meetings*

Shortly after the incorporator files the Articles of Incorporation, he or she should conduct an organizational meeting to empower the corporation to conduct business and provide limited liability. To raise the corporate veil, the business must look and act like a corporation. Generally, this requires the business to follow corporate formalities. If organizational meetings are not conducted and formalities are not followed, persons who believe they are acting through the corporation may incur personal obligations and liabilities. Conducting the organizational meetings promptly and properly lays the foundation for an impermeable corporate veil.

The Articles of Incorporation may have provided the names of the corporation's initial Directors and Officers; however, the incorporator must perform corporate formalities to effectuate the Articles of Incorporation after they are filed. In the incorporator's organizational meeting, he or she should elect the Director(s), present the Articles of Incorporation, and present a proposed form of Bylaws for the corporation.

*For examples of organizational minutes, see the Corporate Forms disk available with the Using Your Own Corporation series.*

Immediately following the incorporator's organizational meeting, and within sixty days after the incorporator files the Articles of Incorporation, the Director(s) should conduct an organizational meeting to establish the corporation's structure and powers. To establish proper corporate formalities, the Director(s) organizational meeting should be recorded in minutes of the meeting. The Director(s) organizational meeting should roughly follow the following agenda:

1. Presentation, acceptance, and approval of the Articles of Incorporation;
2. Approval and acceptance of action taken at previous meetings (the incorporator's meeting);
3. Approval and acceptance of the corporation's Bylaws;

4. Approval and acceptance of the corporate seal;

5. Approval and acceptance of the form of share certificate;

6. Authorization to issue shares of stock;

5. Acceptance of share subscriptions as presented to the corporation for the purchase of shares (this determines who the Shareholders will be);

8. Authorization to pay expenses in connection with the formation of the corporation;

9. Election of corporate Officers; and

10. Acceptance of bank resolutions (determines in which financial institution the corporate funds will be kept).

While conducting organizational meetings is an important start in the process of raising and maintaining the corporate veil, it will not alone prevent others from later piercing the veil. To ensure that the corporation can serve its function of providing limited liability, all actors within the corporation must always treat it as the separate legal entity that it is supposed to be. Only by diligently maintaining corporate formalities may you maintain the corporate veil.

## *Providing Management for the Corporation*

### *Step 3: Provide the Corporation with Competent Initial Management*

A corporation is a separate legal entity with a life of its own, but it cannot survive without support. A corporation's management plots the course the corporation will take, makes daily business decisions, and acts as the corporation's voice. Management is often divided among many actors, consisting of the corporation's Directors and Officers. Through their various roles, Directors and Officers maintain and guide the corporation's life and activities.

*For a checklist to use in determining whether an individual should serve on the corporation's Board of Directors, see Using Your Own Corporation disk.*

**Directors**

Shareholders elect all Directors except for the initial Directors to serve as the governing body of the corporation pursuant to the corporation's Bylaws. Often, the Articles of Incorporation provide the minimum and maximum number of Directors, and the Bylaws or a resolution of the Board of Directors will set the exact number of Directors. Some states impose a minimum number of Directors, but many, including Wyoming and Nevada, allow one Director to run a corporation. Some states require the Directors to be Shareholders in the corporation, but most do not. The form and composition of the Board of Directors may affect the operation of the corporation.

The Board of Directors is comprised of the individual Directors. Its meetings are conducted pursuant to the Bylaws and are generally directed by the Chairman of the Board. The Board of Directors may be divided into committees to meet certain needs or provide certain services for the corporation, such as auditing, compensation, and/or nomination of potential Officers. The corporation's size and the nature of its business determine whether committees are necessary. If the corporation has a modest beginning, it may be appropriate to have only one Director on the Board, who may serve in other roles for the corporation.

Corporations take many approaches in determining the composition of the Board of Directors. The Board should include a broad spectrum of members with a wide variety of experience and diverse problem-solving talents. Generally, a Board of Directors consists of representatives of senior management, outside independent business people, perhaps someone from the community, and in some cases, the corporation's principal outside legal counsel and even its banker. However, the composition may vary drastically. Although the structure and composition of corporations' Boards of Directors may vary, all Boards generally serve the same function in corporate management.

The Board of Directors holds an enormous amount of power and control over the corporation. It sets corporate policy, actively manages the affairs of the business, and selects and supervises the corporation's Officers. Directors can call meetings among themselves, sign contracts binding the corporation to various obligations, conduct purchases and sales of various assets, and incur debts in the corporation's name. They can appoint and terminate the Officers at any time, upon a majority vote of the Directors. Directors can regulate the sale and transfer of the corporation's shares, including the price for purchases and sales. They can also control the corporation's bank account, including who mayor may not sign checks. Accordingly, careful selection of Directors is essential to a corporation's success.

Directors owe various duties to the corporation, including fiduciary duties and duties of care and loyalty. In Delaware, Directors are also under a statutory duty to fully and fairly disclose all material information when seeking Shareholder action. While Directors' duties are commonly referred to as duties to the Shareholders, they are more accurately described as duties to the overall corporation. Each Director owes duties to Shareholders, unions, creditors, or anyone contractually related to the corporation.

Corporate controversies in the recent past highlighted Directors' and Officers' responsibilities, and may well cause change in the consequences for Directors and Officers who fail to fulfill their duties. To mitigate the fiduciary duties a Director owes to the corporation, Directors may be indemnified in either the Articles of Incorporation or the corporation's Bylaws. The continuing effect of such indemnification is uncertain in light of recent events. The Directors' duties of care and loyalty limit and guide the Directors' actions, and may be enforced by Shareholders. Directors and Officers liability insurance is also available to protect Directors and Officers and encourage their participation in the corporation. Despite current uncertainty, Directors' duties and the rights of individual Directors should be considered when choosing Directors for the corporation._

## Officers

A corporation's Officers may consist of a Chief Executive Officer, President, Vice President, Secretary, Treasurer, General Manager, Controller or Chief Financial Officer, and various Assistant Officers; however, the Board of Directors determines the number of Officers, the scope of their responsibility and their compensation. The Directors appoint Officers at the annual Directors meeting. Officers may have many of the powers that Directors possess, but only if the Directors delegate such powers to the Officers. Generally, Officers are responsible for the day-to-day management of the corporation, and may be held accountable under the same duties as Directors. States require corporations to have certain Officers, but may permit one person to act as more than one Officer. For example, Nevada requires a corporation to have a President, Secretary, and Treasurer, but one person can serve in all three positions. The following are the Officers typically used by corporations and their roles within a corporation:

**Chief Executive Officer** - The Chief Executive Officer (CEO) has general supervision over the corporation, presides at all corporate meetings, is often also the Chairman of the Board of Directors, and has the power to sign all corporate documents, share certificates, and other instruments, except where the President must sign by law.

**President** - The President reports directly to the Board of Directors, carries out their requests or any act they authorize, and is ultimately responsible for the actions of the corporation's other Officers. The President's power is limited to matters that arise within the ordinary course of business and are in the best interests of the corporation. The President may also be the Chief Executive Officer and may substitute for the Chairman of the Board of Directors in his or her absence.

**Vice President** - The Vice President acts as an assistant to the President and may be assigned an important role in corporate administration. In the event of the President's absence, death, or incapacity, the Vice President may assume the President's power and duties and act in his or her place; however, the Vice President has no other powers by virtue of the office and generally cannot bind the corporation.

**Corporate Secretary** - The Secretary ensures that the corporation's actions are properly authorized and documented. Generally, the Secretary is the one to prepare resolutions, which he or she brings to either a Board of Directors or Shareholders meeting to be read and voted on. The character of the corporation's business and the relative power of other Officers generally determine the scope of the Secretary's authority, but his or her powers may overlap with those of the Treasurer, Controller, or Auditor. The Secretary also may serve as the liaison between corporate management and the Shareholders.

**Treasurer** - The Treasurer is responsible for all financial records and transactions, including maintaining the corporation's bank accounts, investments, and liabilities. The Treasurer' usual powers include maintaining, caring for, and exercising custody over corporate funds and securities, maintaining books of accounts and records, preparing financial statements, and disbursing corporate funds. The Treasurer's information allows the Board of Directors to make informed decisions regarding the corporation's financial future.

**General Manager** - The General Manager acts as necessary in the usual course of the corporation's business. The General Manager's specific functions vary with the size and nature of the corporation. His or her authority may be limited to general management over specific portions of the corporation's business, such as sales or manufacturing.

**Controller** - Generally, the Controller is the chief accounting officer who works with any audit committee, outside auditors, creditors, and the corporate counsel. The Controller's powers may include maintaining and auditing the corporation's financial records, preparing financial statements, and supervising company accounting practices. The Controller position may also be entitled as the Chief Financial Officer (CFO).

**Assistant Officers** - Assistant Officers perform the specific duties assigned to them by Directors and senior Officers, and they may substitute for senior Officers during absences.

As indicated above, each Officer owes duties to the corporation he or she serves. With the aforementioned powers come responsibilities for each Officer. By following corporate formalities and acting in accordance with their duties to the corporation, Directors and Officers may protect themselves and the Shareholders from personal liability.

## *Issuing the Corporation's Shares of Stock*

### *Step 4: Determine Ownership of the Corporation and Acquire Financing*

Upon the corporation's formation, it is authorized to issue up to the amount and types of stock specified in its Articles of Incorporation. Depending upon the incorporator's plan for the corporation, the corporation may have a single class of stock or multiple classes of stock providing different rights to their owners (classes or types of stock include common stock and various forms of preferred stock).

While the amount and types of stock may be altered at a later date, doing so requires some extra effort. Accordingly, prudent use of the corporation's initial stock (the authorized stock) will simplify future transactions and allow the corporation to avoid potential problems.

Most businesses hoping to grow soon and steadily should start with 25 million to 50 million shares of authorized common stock and distribute them prudently. It is important to note that all distributions or sales of stock require that the corporation comply with regulations promulgated by the Securities and Exchange Commission. Each of the various stages of distribution will pose different challenges and requirements.

Regardless of the type of stock issued or the nature of the equity offering through which the Shareholder obtains his or her interest, it is important to remember at all times that the Shareholders own the corporation. They have the right to vote for Directors and vote on certain corporate decisions. If the Directors decide to distribute corporate profits, Shareholders have the right to receive such distributions.

Corporations should take care in the issuance of shares of stock to potential Shareholders, because Shareholders may play a significant role in the corporation's activities. Issuing corporate shares of stock provides the corporation with financial resources, but the financial resources are obtained in exchange for ownership of the corporation. Developing corporations should be especially cautious about giving up too much control by selling shares of stock. While venture capitalists' financial resources may be appealing, by taking too much money and selling too much stock, you could give someone else control of the corporation. Prudent use of the corporation's stock will prevent a loss of control and ensure that the corporation has esources necessary for future financing needs.

Competent use of securities requires much more guidance than provided above; however, such material is beyond the scope of this book. A basic review of these issues is found in "Writing Winning Business Plans" by Garrett Sutton.

# III. Maintaining the Veil by Maintaining Corporate Formalities

By properly forming a corporation and engaging in initial formalities, a veil is raised that may protect Shareholders, Officers and Directors from personal liability and provide tax benefits. However, to ensure that the corporate veil remains intact and the business meets its potential, all persons involved in the corporation must follow certain corporate formalities. Limited liability and tax benefits are not rights granted to every businessperson, but privileges earned by following corporate formalities. The following nine rules provide general guidance for maintaining the corporate veil while conducting business through a corporation:

1. Perform all Annual filings;
2. Maintain Internal Formalities, including resident agent;
3. Maintain a Written Record of Corporate Decisions;
4. Provide the World with Corporate Notice;
5. Ensure the Corporation is Sufficiently Capitalized;
6. Maintain the Distinction Between Corporate Assets and Personal Assets; and
7. Use Caution when Distributing Corporate Profits.
8. Separate Bank Accounts
9. Separate Tax Return

Although the burden of maintaining corporate formalities may not be appealing, the consequences of neglecting corporate formalities are great. Whether the corporation has followed the foregoing rules becomes important when a creditor seeks to receive payment through the assets of the corporation's individual Shareholder, Director, or Officer. Each rule and its various implications are discussed in more depth below. Additionally, we will review the rules and the implications of failing to follow the rules when we consider cases from seventeen states involving corporate veil piercing issues.

### *Performing Annual Filings*

Annual filings are required to protect and ensure the longevity of the corporation. In addition to the permits, licenses, or approvals that are unique to the corporation's business, every corporation must obtain and maintain a corporate charter in good standing. In many states, a corporation must file an annual report, providing the names and addresses of Officers and Directors, and annual fees. If such filings are not completed in a timely fashion, the state may revoke the corporate charter and the corporation will cease to exist. The time, energy, and expense expended organizing the corporation will be wasted if the state revokes the corporate charter. While it may be possible to have the charter reinstated, the best way to maintain the corporate veil and ensure that the corporation serves its purpose is to simply perform annual filings in a timely manner.

### *Maintaining Internal Formalities*

Bylaws adopted by the Directors in their organizational meeting provide the guidelines for the corporation's future actions and corporate policy. Specifically, the Bylaws should provide the following:

1. Notice requirements for Directors meetings;
2. The minimum number of annual Directors meetings;
3. The date for annual Shareholders meetings;
4. The requirements for special Shareholders meetings;

5. The responsibilities of each Officer and Director; The procedures for removing Officers or Directors;

6. The procedures for Shareholders' inspection of the corporation's records; and

7. The name and address of the corporation's resident agent.

Although they shape the internal operations of the corporation, Bylaws should not be complicated or provide intricate procedures. Necessity determines the extent and detail provided in the corporation's Bylaws, which may be amended, altered, or repealed by the Board of Directors.

All decisions the corporation makes and all actions the corporation takes should be in compliance with the rules established by the Bylaws. Compliance with the Bylaws indicates that the corporation's Directors, Officers, and Shareholders treat the corporation as a separate entity with its own rights and limitations. If the Directors, Officers, and Shareholders treat the corporation as a separate entity, courts will be less likely to ignore the division between corporate property and the rights of the individual Directors, Officers, and Shareholders. The corporate veil will be maintained.

As well, in most states it is imperative to have a current resident agent to accept service of process. Failure to have a resident agent in place can lead to arguments that the corporate veil should be pierced.

### *Maintain a Written Record of Corporate Decisions*

Even if a small group of people or a single person controls the corporation, it should conduct meetings and prepare records of such meetings. Shareholders and Directors conduct three types of meetings, which should each be recorded through minutes of meetings. As provided above, immediately following incorporation, **organizational meetings** should be conducted. During the corporation's life, **regular meetings** must be conducted annually pursuant to the corporation's Bylaws to reflect elections and the corporation's other decisions. Additionally, a corporation may hold special meetings when called by the Directors or Shareholders. Special meetings are held to discuss urgent items of business or to approve any legal or tax issues. The general procedure for conducting Directors or Shareholders meetings is provided below.

Prior to a meeting of Shareholders, all Shareholders must receive or waive notice of the meeting. Prior to a Directors' meeting, all Directors must receive or waive notice of the meeting. In meetings of Shareholders or Directors, corporate formalities require voting and an official record of actions taken at the meeting. The official record of actions taken in regular meetings, as well as the organizational meetings, is provided as the minutes of the meeting. Minutes provide a record of the corporation's resolutions. A resolution is a document that records actions that the Directors or Shareholders "resolve" to take on the corporation's behalf. The nature and timing of the corporation's decisions dictate whether a resolution or minutes of a meeting provide an appropriate record of a decision.

An alternative in most states to conducting actual meetings and preparing minutes for those meetings is for the corporation to authorize action by written consent. This is the quickest and easiest way to document formal corporate action. Directors and/or Shareholders sign a document that contains the language of the corporation's decision or resolution. By signing the document, the Directors and/or Shareholders approve the decision or resolution. To ensure that an action by written consent is adequately documented, all Directors and/or Shareholders must sign the consent form. The corporation should keep signed consent forms in the corporate minute book.

By conducting the necessary meetings and preparing adequate records, a corporation provides documentation to protect the corporate veil. Should a creditor seek to pierce the corporate veil at a later date, the corporation's records will serve as evidence of its separate existence. In addition, maintaining proper records may help to avoid future miscommunications and misunderstandings within the corporation.

Although many people believe that preparing annual meeting minutes is difficult, the minor inconvenience is greatly outweighed by the potential problems that failing to prepare such records could cause. If necessary, a service provider may prepare the required minutes for the corporation for a reasonable fee. Our firm charges $150 per year to prepare minutes. You may call toll free 1-800-700-1430 for more information.

### *Providing the World with Corporate Notice*

Whenever the corporation enters into a contract or engages in any business activity whatsoever, it must do so clearly as a corporation. Individual Officers or Directors may be subject to personal liability if they act on the corporation's behalf, but fail to clearly indicate that they are acting in their capacity as the corporation's Officer or Director. To avoid creditors or others from piercing the corporate veil and attacking individual members of the corporation's management or Shareholders, it must be clear that the corporation, and not an individual, is acting. Business cards, letterhead, invoices, company checks, brochures, etc ... must identify the corporation. The full name of the corporation should be provided (not XYZ, but XYZ, Inc.). All contracts and correspondences signed by Directors or Officers for the corporation should be signed with reference to their corporate designation. If the corporation takes steps to ensure that others know that the corporation, and not an individual Officer or Director is acting, the corporate veil will be more resistant to attack.

### *Avoiding Under-Capitalization*

Although most jurisdictions will not allow creditors to pierce the corporate veil solely because the corporation had insufficient assets, the risk of veil piercing provides reason to ensure that the corporation is sufficiently capitalized. California and few other states have relied on undercapitalization in piercing corporate veils. A corporation should have sufficient resources to meet its short-term obligations whether it is just starting, is part of a cooperative project, or is merely one element in a greater corporate strategy. If the corporation is undercapitalized, a creditor may argue, and a court could accept the argument, that the corporation exists simply to help its owners shelter their assets. As is discussed further below, this may be enough reason for a court to pierce the corporate veil and find personal liability for Officers, Directors, and/or Shareholders.

### *Maintaining the Distinction between Corporate and Personal Assets*

A common but fatal mistake for developing corporations occurs when its management and/or Shareholders fail to maintain the distinction between corporate and personal assets. Whether arising from loans from the corporation to individuals, shared bank accounts, shared tax returns, or individual use of corporation property, failure to separate corporate assets from personal assets negates the corporation's separate identity. To prevent creditors from piercing the corporate veil, the corporation must maintain a separate bank account, file separate tax returns, and use corporate assets only for corporate purposes.

The corporation should not be used as a lender for its Officers, Directors or Shareholders. An air of impropriety is created when a corporation loans money to members of management, even if management genuinely intends to repay the loan. The infamous chain of corporate scandals in spring and summer 2002 highlighted the dangers involved in loaning to management, as such loans were often cited in allegations that a Director or Officer breached their fiduciary duties. The best way for the corporation to avoid potential problems is to refuse to lend money to its Directors and Officers.

Regardless of their personal interest or role in the corporation, nobody should treat the corporation's property as personal property. By clearly distinguishing between corporate and personal assets, the corporation may indicate and retain its separate identity. By reporting and maintaining the corporate assets separately from management's or Shareholders' personal assets, the corporation will reduce the potential for successful lawsuits against Officers, Directors, and individual Shareholders.

### *Cautiously Distributing Corporate Profits*

Whether a corporation distributes its profits through dividends paid to shareholders or compensation paid to employees, the corporation's distribution of profits may provide a basis for creditors to pierce the corporate veil. The veil that limits the liability of Shareholders, Directors, and Officers also creates limitations on the corporation's ability to pay such corporate actors from the corporation's profits. If the corporation fails to obey established rules for the distribution of corporate profits, a creditor may use such failure as an indication that the corporate actors are not treating the corporation as a separate legal entity. To reduce creditors' ability to pierce the corporate veil, the corporation must exercise caution in distributing its profits.

Every state authorizes a corporation's Board of Directors to issue dividends to its Shareholders. However, the Directors' decision to declare dividends may result in substantial fines assessed against the individual Directors if the dividend is found to be illegal. Dividends from surplus cannot exceed limits established by reference to the corporation's assets. "Nimble" dividends, or dividends paid from profits, may be issued when the corporation's surplus is insufficient. However, such dividends may only be paid when such payment does not impair the capital representing preferred stock. Directors must determine whether the corporation has sufficient funds legally available to pay dividends to protect themselves from potential liability. To avoid liability arising from the issuance of dividends, corporations should consult with legal counsel before deciding to issue dividends.

### *Separate Bank Account*

A corporate veil will be pierced in cases where the company founders use a personal bank account for business affairs. You cannot consistently pay business expenses from a personal account and, conversely, you cannot pay personal expenses from a company bank account. Failure to follow these simple guidelines can be catastrophic, so as soon as you incorporate obtain an EIN (Employer Identification Number) from the IRS and use it to open a corporate bank account.

### *Separate Tax Return*

Because you have obtained an EIN for your entity you must now file a separate tax return with the IRS. Fear not, this is your chance to take all the deductions you may be entitled to take. But failure to file a separate return can lead to claims that you are not following corporate formalities. So file - and take advantage of the tax benefits you are entitled to in the first place.

Many developing corporations do not have sufficient assets or profits to distribute dividends to Shareholders, but they must compensate Officers, Directors, or other employees for their services. Especially in start-up businesses, the compensation a corporation pays to Officers, Directors, and other employees may determine the corporation's ability to succeed. Equity compensation (using shares of the corporation's stock, stock options, or other alternative forms of compensation) may be attractive. Compensation based in part on the corporation's profits may also be appealing. However, all forms of compensation should be based primarily upon the market value of the employee's services. The Internal Revenue Service may scrutinize excessive compensation paid to Directors, Officers, or employees and decide to tax excessive compensation as dividends.

Corporations that over-compensate their employees may create liability for the Directors based on Shareholders' claims of mismanagement, breach of fiduciary duties, self-dealing, or waste of corporate assets. Through a derivative action, the Shareholders may regain control of the corporation and its assets. The corporation may then assert legal claims against former Directors, creating personal liability for such Directors. To avoid potential liability based on employee compensation and excessive tax liability, Directors must ensure that compensation paid by the corporation is reasonable.

All decisions regarding the distribution of a corporation's profits or compensation for employees is subject to the discretion of the Board of Directors. However, to avoid potential liability for the corporation and for themselves, Directors must carefully consider the effects of every use of the corporation's assets. Caution and the advice of legal counsel may be necessary to prevent the Board's distribution decisions from creating unwanted liability.

# IV. Conducting Shareholders Meetings

Generally, annual Shareholders meetings must be conducted to elect and appoint the corporation's Director(s) for the ensuing year. In addition, Shareholders meetings must be conducted prior to a sale or merger of the corporation, and as provided in the corporation's Bylaws. Certain procedures and defined terms guide a corporation's decisions in a Shareholders meeting.

Before a meeting may be conducted, all Shareholders must be provided with written notice of the meeting, which should specify the time, place, date, and purpose of the meeting. The corporation's Bylaws should provide the specific time frame for the required notice, but the notice must be reasonable and usually must be provided not less than 10 days nor more than 60 days before the meeting. Alternatively, in some states a meeting may be held if all Shareholders sign a document waiving notice of the meeting.

While any business may be conducted in a regular meeting of the Shareholders, special meetings are limited in scope. The notice of a special meeting provided to Shareholders provides the specific purpose and scope of the meeting. No other business may be transacted at a special meeting unless all Shareholders are present or represented by proxy and consent to the additional decisions. This provides reason to ensure that all potential concerns are included in the notice of a special meeting.

In some states of incorporation, such as Wyoming and Nevada, a corporation's Shareholders meetings may be conducted anywhere in the world. While the timing of the annual meeting is prescribed by statute and the corporation's Bylaws, special meetings may be held whenever they are needed, provided that the notice requirement is satisfied. Because some states allow Shareholders meetings to be conducted anywhere, and to be paid for by the corporation as a business expense, annual meetings may provide Shareholders with a tax-free vacation. Of course, the expenses involved in conducting such meeting should be reasonable to avoid wasting the corporation's assets.

In addition to satisfying the notice requirement, a corporation must have a quorum present before it may hold a Shareholders meeting. A quorum is the minimum number of shares required to be present at a meeting for the Shareholders to conduct corporate business. While the corporation's Bylaws determine the number required to establish a quorum, generally, at least one-half of the shares issued and outstanding are required for the Shareholders to conduct a meeting. The shares satisfying the quorum requirement may be represented by Shareholders personally attending the meeting and Shareholders represented by proxy.

*For a sample proxy authorization, see Using Your Own Corporation*

A proxy is a Shareholder's written authorization directing another to vote the Shareholder's shares at a Shareholders meeting. The proxy holder, which is the person directed to vote for the absent Shareholder, votes the shares in the manner directed by the absent Shareholder. As indicated above, a quorum may consist of present Shareholders and shares represented by proxy.

Additional procedural details of Shareholders meetings may be provided in the corporation's Bylaws. These include the number of votes required to pass a proposed resolution and other important considerations necessary for conducting business. As mentioned above, however, not all Bylaws provide the same level of detail. They should at least provide framework through which the corporation can make decisions, including decisions made through Shareholders meetings.

# V. Conducting Directors Meetings

The details of the procedures involved in conducting Directors meetings and Shareholders meetings are both provided in the corporation's Bylaws, and are generally the same. Annual Directors meetings must be conducted to elect Officers to serve for the ensuing year. Additionally, Directors meetings should be conducted whenever a key legal, tax, or financial decision is made. Such decisions include the following:

- Opening bank accounts;
- Entering into written employment agreements;
- Entering into Shareholder agreements;
- Making tax elections, such as an election for S corporation status;
- Amending the corporation's Articles of Incorporation or Bylaws;
- Purchasing or selling a business;
- Forming subsidiaries;
- Purchasing, selling, or leasing property to be used by the corporation, including office buildings, computer systems, company cars, or other items;
- Acquiring loans or financing or issuing bonds;
- Conducting reorganizations, including mergers;
- Declaring stock splits or dividends;
- Approving plans of merger, liquidation, or dissolution;
- Enacting employee benefit plans, including pension and profit sharing plans, health insurance plans, stock option plans, and others;

- Settling lawsuits and claims or indemnifying Officers or Directors;
- Issuing shares of the corporation's stock or granting warrants or options;
- Changing the corporation's registered agent or registered office;
- Filling vacancies on the Board of Directors or replacing Officers;
- Authorizing the corporation to enter into certain contracts;
- Establishing committees or appointing Directors to serve on committees;
- Redeeming or retiring corporate shares of stock;
- Deciding salary or compensation of corporate Officers; and
- Ratifying prior corporate acts made by Officers or Directors.

In conducting Directors meetings to make decisions on any of the foregoing issues, the corporation must satisfy notice requirements and maintain a record of the Board of Directors' decisions. By doing so, the corporation will show the proper level of deference and respect to individual Directors and will demonstrate its obedience to its Bylaws. The corporation will not only be functioning like a corporation, but it will also look like a corporation so as to maintain the corporate veil.

# VI. The Limits of the Corporate Veil

## *Protecting Shareholders from Liability*

The corporate veil shields Shareholders from personal liabilities arising from the corporation's debts, obligations, or actions. Corporations that engage in the corporate formalities discussed above and consistently maintain such corporate formalities should be able to retain the corporate veil and protect Shareholders. If the corporate veil endures, each Shareholder may lose only that which they invested in the corporation. The corporation's additional debts or obligations will not affect the Shareholders, except by limiting their ability to recover their investment before or upon the dissolution of the corporation. The most a Shareholder will lose is that which they invested.

If the corporate veil is pierced, Shareholders' limited liability may be lost. Instead of protecting the Shareholders' personal assets, the corporation and its activities would become a source of personal liability for the Shareholders. If, for example, the corporation owed another business for services or goods delivered to the corporation, and the corporation became unable to satisfy its debts, the business could attempt to collect money from the individual Shareholders.

*States differ in the approaches they take to piercing the corporate veil. As discussed below, failing to follow corporate formalities is one of many considerations courts may make. Many courts also require evidence of fraud.*

Imagine that Jim Jones was the only Shareholder of XYZ, Inc. XYZ, Inc., had borrowed money from Syndicated Lending, Inc. When Syndicated Lending, Inc., sought to collect from XYZ, Inc., after it defaulted on its loan, Syndicated Lending, Inc., found that XYZ, Inc., had no assets. However, Syndicated Lending, Inc., discovered that the Shareholder, Jim Jones, had a small fortune and an expensive home. Syndicated Lending, Inc., further discovered that XYZ, Inc.'s Directors, who had since disappeared, had failed to follow corporate formalities. Accordingly, Syndicated Lending, Inc., sought to pierce XYZ, Inc.'s corporate veil. Because XYZ, Inc., failed to follow corporate formalities, Syndicated Lending, Inc., may be able to use Jones's home and other assets to satisfy the XYZ, Inc.'s debts. Whether such an attempt is successful will depend on state law and the specific facts of each case. But you don't want to be put in such a position ...

To protect Shareholders from personal liability for the corporation's debts and obligations, the corporation must follow corporate formalities. By taking the time and expending the minimum energy necessary to maintain the corporate veil, the corporation ensures that it will serve the function for which it was intended.

## *Protecting Directors and Officers from Liability*

Generally, Directors and Officers are not personally liable for the liabilities and obligations of the corporation that they serve. However, the role of Directors and Officers within a corporation subjects them to numerous restrictions and duties that may provide alternate basis for liability. Directors' and Officers' duties of loyalty, care, and full disclosure may provide the basis for personal liability if a Director or Officer breaches his or her duties. Such breach may also alter management of the corporation through a Shareholders derivative action. Additionally, a Director or Officer who is found to be using the corporation as his or her alter ego may be held liable for the corporation's obligations.

*States' approaches to alter ego vary. For more information, see the state-by-state analysis below.*

Further dissection of Directors' and Officers' duties of loyalty, care, and full disclosure provides guidance for management. The following paragraphs describe the various manifestations of these general duties.

## Duty of Loyalty

The duty of loyalty may be considered somewhat analogous to an employee's covenant to not compete with the corporation. Like employees, Officers and Directors should not engage in practices that endanger the corporation's business. While they are employed, they may not engage in active competition, solicit the corporations' customers or employees, or misuse confidential information or trade secrets. After the employment relationship is terminated, former Directors and Officers may compete, solicit customers, and engage in other competitive activities. Because of the amount of information and power corporations grant to their Officers and Directors, however, Officers' and Directors' duty of loyalty also focuses upon their ability to directly interfere with the corporation's business. The duty of loyalty requires Directors and Officers to apprise the corporation of "corporate opportunities" and receive informed consent before entering into a transaction with the corporation.

*For an example of a corporate veil pierced because of a corporate opportunity, see the Washington case of Howard v. Pidgeon.*

A "corporate opportunity" is any investment, purchase, lease or other any other opportunity that is in the corporation's nature, in the line of the corporation's business and is of practical advantage to it. It is illegal for a Director or Officer to embrace such opportunity if, by doing so, his or her self-interest will be brought into conflict with the corporation's self-interest. Some jurisdictions also limit Directors and Officers' ability to appropriate corporate opportunities. During their time in office, a Director or Officer may discover opportunities for the corporation. The Director of Officer may have personal business opportunities that are somehow related to the corporation's business. The corporation will be able to pursue some of the opportunities the Director or Officer discovers for the corporation, others it will not. The scope of the corporation's business, the reasonable expectations of key actors, the way in which the Director or Officer learned of the opportunity, and the corporation's ability to pursue the opportunity may determine which opportunities a Director or Officer may personally pursue.

Although there are no certain guidelines for determining which opportunities belong to the corporation, controversy and liability may be avoided if Directors and Officers use caution regarding corporate opportunities. Even when a corporation seems to lack the requisite resources, some courts require a Director or Officer to first offer the opportunity to the corporation. Resignation before completion of the questionable activity may not constitute a defense to liability arising from a corporate opportunity, as courts have found liability even where Directors and Officers resigned before the completion of the transaction. To pursue such opportunities, Directors and Officers should (i) fully disclose all material facts concerning the opportunity and his or her interest in them and obtain the corporation's consent to the actions, (ii) be able to show that the corporation was unable to take advantage of the corporate opportunity because it was insolvent or otherwise legally disabled from pursuing it, or (iii) be able to show that the corporation abandoned the corporate opportunity.

The duty of loyalty also requires Directors and Officers to either avoid or use great caution in transactions involving conflicts of interest. Conflicts may arise through the compensation paid to management or in transactions between a Director or Officer and the corporation. Before deciding upon compensation for any Director or Officer, the Board of Directors should ensure that the compensation is fair. Courts will scrutinize a compensation decision closely, especially if the recipient participated in it. If a court finds that the Board of Directors approved excessive compensation, it may prevent the corporation from honoring the arrangement. Courts have not sustained challenges to compensation arrangements merely because the recipients voted as Directors to approve them, but the Director or Officer's abstention would improve the chances that the recipient would prevail. A Director or Officer may defeat challenges through a majority vote or pursuant to the decision of other "interested" Directors, thorough disclosure of the nature of the interest or Shareholder approval.

Transactions between a corporation and its Directors, Officers, or Shareholders, or which otherwise benefit a corporate actor, are a great source of criticism, but may be conducted safely and beneficially. The role of corporate actors may lead to assumptions of impropriety, but formalities may counteract such assumptions and protect both the corporation and individuals from potential liability arising from such transactions. Transactions between a corporation and a corporate actor may be conducted safely as arms length transactions. Any individual corporate actor who engages in a transaction with the corporation or who may receive a personal benefit from the corporation's action must remember that the corporation is a separate legal entity and that the Board of Directors owes duties to the Shareholders.

To protect the corporate actor and the corporation, such transactions must be conducted procedurally and substantively as if the corporate actor did not have any relation to the corporation. Agreements must be made under the same terms and with the same formalities as if the corporate actor was not related to the corporation in any way. The Director or Officer will have the burden of proving that the transaction was fair if problems arise.

In practice, it may seem difficult to ignore the contributions of a corporate actor when conducting a business transaction. If, for example, the corporation's general manager, Jim Jones, helped to develop a new product and later wanted to independently develop an application of the product, he would have to negotiate the terms of his use of the product as if he was not part of the corporation. Jones would have to negotiate and enter into a written agreement with the corporation for his use of the product under terms that are fair to the corporation and which do not recognize his prior contributions to the product. After all, Jones's prior contributions were made by him as part of the corporation, not as an individual. Only by treating Jim Jones as a stranger may the corporation protect itself from potential liability. Jim Jones and all other corporate actors must be kept at arm's length from the corporation throughout such transactions.

## Duty of Care

Directors and Officers must discharge their responsibilities with "due care," which is often described as that degree of care that an ordinarily prudent person in a like position would exercise under similar circumstances. However, not all cases of mistaken judgment constitute a breach of the duty of care. The "business judgment rule" encourages businesses and management to take risks by insulating Directors and Officers from liability unless their decisions reflect "gross negligence" or "recklessness." Simple mistakes generally will not create liability. Courts may still hold Directors and Officers liable for making decisions without adequately investigating other solutions or adequately supervising decision makers. The Directors and Officers liability may be limited through the Articles of Incorporation, but corporate records are also helpful to prevent Directors or Officers from incurring liability for a breach of their duty of care.

## Duties of Full Disclosure and Candor

Directors and Officers owe duties of full disclosure and candor to the corporation's Shareholders, which usually arise in the context of the Board of Directors submitting matters to Stockholders for a vote. Such duties require the Board to fully and fairly disclose all material information within the Board's control whenever it seeks Shareholder action. If the Directors fail to disclose all germane facts to the Shareholders, the Directors may be liable for breaching their duties of full disclosure and candor. To ensure that these duties are fulfilled, Directors and Officers should volunteer information to Shareholders truthfully and candidly.

Certain key events have revealed the importance of not only full disclosure, but also accurate disclosure. The acts of AIG, Goldman Sachs, and others spurred greater scrutiny in the investment community. In response, reforms aimed at increasing corporate transparency have been discussed and will likely change some corporate practices. However, simply meeting government imposed reporting requirements is not enough. To protect the corporation and ensure a healthy working relationship between management and Shareholders, every member of the corporation should acknowledge that the Shareholders are the corporation's owners and are entitle to know about everything that the corporation does. Partial or eventual disclosure from management to the Shareholders is not enough.

## Additional Duties

In addition to the duties of loyalty, care, good faith, and full disclosure Directors owe to Shareholders, Directors owe duties to the communities the corporation may affect. Statutory duties create a potential for criminal or civil liability based on a Director's activities within the corporation. These include laws governing the sale of securities, environmental and occupational health and safety, use of intellectual property, trade practices, and more. While the corporate veil may protect Directors and Officers from some forms of personal liability, they must be aware of the many limitations on their activities conducted through the corporation.

Notable events in American businesses have demonstrated the potential for liability for corporate Directors' and Officers' for their violations of duties to Shareholders and statutory duties. Because of public disgust with the management practices of businesses such as Lehman Brothers, AIG and Countrywide, the duties owed by Directors and Officers and the consequences of violating such duties are in a state of transition. While some are crying for the creation of more statutory duties, others suggest reaffirming ethical practices by simply revising MBA programs. Others have more calmly suggested that the actions of a few score of bad apples should not be turned into an indictment of the entire business establishment. Nevertheless, when the lawmakers get involved and pass the Sarbanes-Oxley and Dodd-Frank Financial Reform bills and the courts must later interpret what was meant, Directors and Officers should consult with legal counsel to stay abreast of shifting requirements and avoid personal liability for breaching a duty they may not know that they have.

### Corporations vs. LLCs

With the increasing popularity and utility of Limited Liability Companies, many have asked whether an LLC veil can be pierced. As well, many promoters trying to sell LLCs have represented that LLCs, as different entity creatures, will not have their veil pierced. Alas, this is not accurate.

LLC veils are being pierced, as we knew they would. A strong statement from the Wyoming Supreme Court articulates the landscape:

> "If the members and officers of an LLC fail to treat it as a separate entity as contemplated by statute, they should not enjoy immunity from individual liability for the LLC's acts that cause damage to third parties. Most, if not all, of the expert LLC commentators have concluded the doctrine of piercing the veil should apply LLC's." citing Kacyee Land Livestock v. Flahive, 2002 WY 73, 46 P.3d 323, 327-328 (Wyo. 2002)."

### State Differences

Some states are more likely to pierce the corporate veil than others, which is why we have reviewed a sampling of state cases for you to consider. As well, in some states veil piercing cases are brought more often. The top five states in order of most cases filed are New York, California, Texas, Ohio and Pennsylvania. See Peter B. Oh, Veil-Piercing at 25, 35 n.194 (2010). As you would expect, the filings reflect population density. But they also reflect the states in which the strategy may be successful. Interestingly, Mr. Oh found that on a national basis 48.51% of veil piercing cases were successful, which is all the more reason to be cautious when dealing with corporate formalities.

## *What to Avoid: Cases of Pierced Corporate Veils*

Although the steps and formalities provided above will prevent creditors from piecing the veil of limited liability corporations may provide, it is important to note that, in practice, states have applied differing standards when deciding whether to pierce the corporate veil. By reviewing cases in which the courts decided to allow the corporate veil to be pierced, one may discover practices that should be avoided and indicators of possible future developments. The following cases are important in the states of discussion, and they each provide some insight into the rationale courts use in determining whether the corporate veil may be pierced. The changing landscape of corporate governance may affect courts' approach to the corporate veil, but the currently existing standards will not likely be lowered. Rather, the existing standards may provide only the starting point of compliance in the future.

Most jurisdictions apply two considerations when determining whether to pierce the corporate veil: (i) whether the corporation is merely the alter ego of its Directors, Officers or Shareholders; and (ii) whether judicial recognition of the corporate entity will serve to further fraud or injustice. Some jurisdictions apply a third consideration; whether the individual against whom personal liability is sought was in control of the corporation. Jurisdictions differ in how they apply these considerations and how they define their "alter ego" doctrine. Courts consider various factors to determine whether the corporation is merely the alter ego of an individual or a parent corporation, but generally look to see whether there is justification to uphold the corporation's existence. Regardless of which jurisdiction a corporation is in, the best way to prevent the corporate veil from being pierced is simply to obey corporate formalities and treat the corporation as if it is a distinct legal entity. If a corporation's management and owners treat it as if it is a corporation, courts will likely do the same.

The following pages discuss the approaches different states have taken to piercing the corporate veil. Veil piercing may be divided into attempts to assert personal liability against individual Shareholders, attempts to assert personal liability against Directors or Officers, attempts to assert liability against a parent corporation for a subsidiary's debts or obligations, and attempts to assert liability arising from contractual obligations or from court judgments arising from other wrongs. Courts that are hesitant to pierce the corporate veil are said to be conservative. Courts that apply flexible standards or appear willing to pierce the corporate veil are said to be lenient. This does not refer to what they will allow corporations to do, but to the proof they require plaintiffs to provide before they will pierce the corporate veil. While many of the considerations courts use to determine whether to pierce the corporate veil are the same, a courts' willingness to pierce the veil differs. Understanding the approach taken in a specific jurisdiction will allow corporate actors to assess the risk in using corporations to limit liability.

## Arizona Cases

Arizona courts have applied their alter ego approach to corporate veil piercing hesitantly, but with such irregularity and inconsistency as to leave it uncertain whether a corporate veil will be pierced in any given case. Arizona's inconsistency arises from its apparent failure to adopt specific factors or indicators that justify disregarding a corporation as an alter ego. The general approach Arizona courts take to veil piercing requires plaintiffs to establish that the corporation is the alter ego of an individual or a parent corporation and that observance of the corporation will sanction a fraud or promote injustice.

In *Bischofshausen, Etc.* v. *D. W Jaquays Mining* & *Equipment Contractors Co.,* an Arizona court reviewed the veil piercing approaches Arizona takes in contractual disputes or tort claims. 700 P.2d 902 (Az. App.1985). Arizona courts generally recognize and uphold the corporate identity and maintain the corporate veil, provided that (i) the business is conducted on a corporate and not a personal basis, and (ii) the enterprise is established on an adequate financial basis. The corporate fiction will be disregarded and the corporate veil pierced:

> " ... when the corporation is the alter ego or business conduit of a person, and when to observe the corporation would work an injustice. The alter ego status is said to exist when there is such a unity of interest and ownership that the separate personalities of the corporation and the owners cease to exist."

*Id.* at 906 (citing *Dietel* v. *Day,* 492 P .2d 455 (Ariz. App. 1972). The *Bischofshausen* court acknowledged that the corporation involved may have been under-capitalized, was substantially controlled by two Shareholders, and had received loans from another corporation controlled by the same Shareholders. Nevertheless, the court refused to find that the corporation was the alter ego of its Shareholders. Instead, the court found that the characteristics the creditor cited to justify piercing the corporate veil were characteristics common among closely held corporations. Accordingly, it appears that Arizona may permit many of the characteristics often used to demonstrate that a corporation is its Shareholders' alter ego.

In addition to demonstrating Arizona courts' flexibility in veil piercing against Shareholders, *Bischofshausen* limited the risk of personal liability for Directors and Officers. To be held personally liable for the corporation's actions in Arizona, Directors or Officers "must participate or have knowledge amounting to acquiescence or be guilty of negligence in the management or supervision of the corporate affairs causing or contributing to the injury." *Id.* at 909. The defendant Officer in *Bischofshausen* avoided personal liability, because the plaintiff failed to sufficiently prove that the Officer engaged in the requisite level of wrongful conduct.

Federal courts have closely followed Arizona's approach to applying liability to Shareholders, Directors and Officers in Arizona cases. In *Keams* v. *Tempe Technical Institute,* the 9th Circuit Court of Appeals applied Arizona's conservative approach to piercing the corporate veil. 993 F. Supp. 714 (9th Cir. 1997). Although the plaintiff in *Keams* alleged that the defendant Shareholders operated the corporation on a personal basis and that the corporation was undercapitalized from its inception, the court refused to pierce the corporate veil. Evidence that the defendant Shareholders and Officers had commingled funds, failed to observe corporate formalities, diverted corporate funds for personal needs, and failed to perform official functions was not determinative, because the lack of corporate formalities was not sufficient, standing alone, to pierce the corporate veil. *Id.* at 723. The Directors and Officers were also able to avoid personal liability for torts committed by the corporation, because the plaintiff failed to sufficiently show that the defendant participated in the tort, had knowledge amounting to acquiescence, or engaged in negligent management and supervision. *Id.* at 725.

*Torts are wrongful acts that result in personal injury or property damage*

Arizona's approach to piercing the corporate veil leaves some uncertainty, because it does not identify specific factors that will lead a court to determine that the corporation is the Shareholders' alter ego. The level of involvement required for a Director or Officer to incur personal liability is also somewhat uncertain. However, it is clear that Arizona courts are more hesitant to pierce the corporate veil and find personal liability than are courts in other jurisdictions. Nevertheless, corporations in Arizona should exercise caution and follow corporate formalities to further reduce the risk that their corporate veil will be pierced.

## California Cases

California leads in the development of flexible veil piercing; however, the extent of that flexibility remains somewhat uncertain. While some cases suggest that California courts will pierce a corporate veil merely because the corporation is undercapitalized, others apply a two-part test to determine whether the corporate veil should be pierced. Regardless of whether undercapitalization may alone justify a court to pierce the corporate veil, California courts are more likely than other courts to ignore a corporate identity and apply personal liability for the corporation's obligations and debts.

In *Sonora Diamond Corp.* v. *Superior Court,* a California court provided the limitations on its desire to pierce the corporate veil. 83 Cal. App. 4th 523 (2000). The court provided that, to pierce the corporate veil, there must be (i) such a unity of interest and ownership between the corporation and its equitable owner that the separate personalities of the corporation and the Shareholder do not in reality exist, and (ii) an inequitable result if the acts in question are treated as those of the corporation alone. *Id.* at 538. The court further provided a list of the factors it would consider in applying its alter ego doctrine to pierce the veil between parent and subsidiary corporations. The list of factors included the following:

1. Commingling of funds and other assets;
2. Identical equitable ownership in the two entities;
3. Use of the same offices and employees;
4. Use of one as a mere shell or conduit for the affairs of the other;
5. Inadequate capitalization;
6. Disregard of corporate formalities;
7. Lack of segregation of corporate records; and
8. Identical directors and officers.

*Id.* "No one characteristic governs, but the courts must look at all the circumstances to determine whether the doctrine should be applied." *Id.* After reviewing the facts of the case, the court in *Sonora* found that no inequitable result would follow from treating the corporation as a separate entity and refused to pierce the corporate veil.

While *Sonora* provided limitations recognized by California courts, California jurisprudence has been somewhat distorted by the holdings of the 9th Circuit Court of Appeals. In *Nilsson, Robbins, Dalgarn, Berliner, Carson* & *Wurst* v. *Louisiana Hydrolec,* the 9th Circuit Court cited California precedent to provide that under-capitalization alone supports piercing a corporate veil in California. 854 F.2d 1538, 1544 (1988). Also see Wechsler v. Mache International Trade, Inc. 486 F.3d 1286, 1295 (Fed. Cir. (2007). "California law is clear that it is incumbent upon the one seeking to pierce the corporate veil to show by evidence that the financial setup of the corporation is just a sham and accomplishes financial injustice". The case found that the corporate veil should not be pierced because corporation was adequately capitalized. Commenters have properly challenged the validity of the 9th Circuit Court's reading of California precedent. *See* Presser, Stephen B., *Piercing the Corporate Veil* (Clark Boardman Callaghan 2004, updated 2010). At best, the cases cited in *Nilsson* indicate that under-capitalization is one of many factors used in deciding whether to pierce a corporate veil.

Although federal courts may have exaggerated California's willingness to pierce the corporate veil, they are correct in finding that California is more lenient than most jurisdictions. Creditors may be able to pierce the corporate veil in California under circumstances that would not justify veil piercing in other jurisdictions. In cases involving individually controlled corporations and tort creditors pursuing thinly capitalized corporations California courts are likely to pierce the corporate veil.

Therefore, corporate actors in California or conducting business in California should exercise great caution in following corporate formalities and treating the corporation like a separate legal entity.

**Colorado Cases**

Colorado courts consider piercing the corporate veil to be a function of equity, which requires courts to carefully consider the facts of each case and balance considerations to determine whether the veil should be pierced. Because courts do not use juries to decide matters of equity, courts are under less pressure to clearly explain the standards they used in determining whether to pierce the corporate veil. While a judge may have to explain the standards to a jury for the jury to make its decision, no such explanation is necessary when a judge decides whether to pierce the corporate veil. This has left little guidance for a corporation seeking to avoid having its corporate veil pierced. However, Colorado courts have at least indicated when they will not pierce the corporate veil.

The basis for Colorado's corporate veil piercing is similar to that used by other jurisdictions, and was briefly described in *Micciche* v. *Billings:*

> Generally, a corporation is treated as a legal entity separate from its Shareholders, thereby permitting Shareholders to commit limited capital to the corporation with the assurance that they will have no personal liability for the corporation's debts. (citations omitted) When, however, the corporate structure is used so improperly that the continued recognition of the corporation as a separate legal entity would be unfair, the corporate entity may be disregarded and corporate principals held liable for the corporation's actions. (citations omitted) Thus, if it is shown that Shareholders used the corporate entity as a mere instrumentality for the transaction of their own affairs without regard to separate and independent corporate existence, or for the purpose of defeating or evading important legislative policy, or in order to perpetrate a fraud or wrong on another, equity will permit the corporate form to be disregarded and will hold the Shareholders personally responsible for the corporation's improper actions.

727 P .2d 367, 372- 73 (Colo. 1986). While this general description of Colorado's approach to veil piercing may be accurate, it is not sufficiently precise to provide corporations with direction.

In *Straub* v. *Mountain Trails Resort,* a Colorado appellate court considered whether to pierce the corporate veil in a case involving allegations of securities fraud. In its decision, the *Straub* court provided some guidance for corporations in Colorado. The court found that the plaintiffs had been provided with corporate notice and that the corporation had been sufficiently capitalized, maintained corporate records, entered into service contracts and received monies due on debts owing to it. Although the court was not explicit in its rationale, it appears that the court refused to pierce the corporate veil because of such considerations. While these considerations are commonly included in an alter ego approach, the Colorado courts have not clearly enunciated their application of an alter ego doctrine. Accordingly, corporations in Colorado have been left to conduct business without any clear directions from the courts.

Although the federal courts may be distorting Colorado state law, they have at least provided some guidance in veil piercing jurisprudence related to parent/subsidiary relationships. In *Skidmore, Owings & Merrill* v. *Canada Life Assurance Co.,* a Colorado federal District Court considered the following factors in deciding whether to pierce a corporate veil:

1. Commingling of funds and other assets;

2. Failure to maintain adequate corporate records or minutes;

3. The nature of the corporation's ownership and control;

4. Absence of corporate assets and under-capitalization;

5. Use of a corporation as a mere shell, instrumentality or conduit of an individual or another corporation;

6. Disregard of legal formalities and the failure to maintain an arms length relationship among related entities; and,

7. Diversion of the corporation's funds or assets to non-corporate uses.

706 F. Supp. 758,760 (D. Colo. 1989). In addition to the foregoing considerations, Colorado federal District Courts have decided that equity will permit a plaintiff to pierce the corporate veil if the plaintiff shows that the parent corporate used the subsidiary's corporate status to perpetuate a fraud or wrong on another. *FDIC* v. *First Interstate Bank, NA.,* 937 F. Supp. 1461, 1467 (D. Colo. 1996). For a plaintiff to pierce the corporate veil, they must provide evidence that shows that the corporate entity "was used to defeat public convenience, or to justify or protect wrong, fraud or crime." *Id.*

A more recent case provides a more unique take on LLCs. In *RSACO LLC v. Resource Support Associates, Inc.*, 208 Fed. Appx. 632, 640 (10th Cir. 2006), the court absent any real evidence indicating fraud or similar wrongdoing, found that where several LLC's "were owned and operated by the same limited number of family members," where "all of the important decisions with respect to each of [these] related entities" were made by one individual and where "corporate formalities were largely ignored in the day-to-day operations of those entities," then each of the related entities could "reasonably be said to be instrumentalities or agents" of their parent entity as well as each other." The LLC (and corporate) veil may be pierced in the unusual Colorado case.

Colorado state courts apply a more flexible approach and have not enunciated a clear veil piercing doctrine. Prudence and the uncertainty that surround veil piercing in Colorado counsel corporations to closely comply with all corporate formalities. As in all jurisdictions, corporations in Colorado should do all that they can to ensure that they look and act like corporations.

## Delaware Cases

Although Delaware is consistently considered the state with the most settled body of law affecting corporations, it provides surprisingly little law on the subject of piercing the corporate veil. Other jurisdictions offer more fully developed case law on the subject, and seem to provide more ways in which the corporate veil may be pierced. At the least, a plaintiff seeking to pierce the corporate veil in Delaware must offer evidence of fraud or something like it. Accordingly, Delaware may provide a firmer corporate veil, but it also provides some degree of uncertainty. The following cases illustrate the requirements for piercing the corporate veil in Delaware.

In *David* v. *Mast,* a Delaware Chancery Court found that the corporate veil could be pierced to allow consumers to recover for fraud committed by the corporation. 1999 Del. Ch. LEXIS 34. Delaware allows the corporate veil to be pierced in cases of legal or equitable fraud, contravention of law, or public wrong. The Court found that the corporation engaged in fraudulent advertising. In doing so, it restated the Delaware approach to piercing the corporate veil:

> The legal test for determining when a corporate form should be ignored in equity cannot be reduced to a single formula that is neither over- nor under-inclusive. Observation of appropriate formalities by those controlling a

> corporation is typically regarded as an important consideration because it demonstrates that those in control of a corporation treated the corporation as a distinct entity and had a reasonable expectation that the conventional attributes of corporateness, including limited liability, would be accorded to it... .. When those formalities are not respected, the legal fiction of corporateness becomes less "real" in the everyday experience of those involved in the firm's operations and any expectation that others would treat it as a distinct, liability-limiting entity becomes less reasonable. Beyond according respect for the formalities some weight, however, the cases inevitably tend to evaluate the specific facts with a standard of "fraud" or "misuse" or some other general term of reproach in mind.

*Id.* at *6-*7 (quoting *Irwin & Leighton* v. *WM Anderson Co.,* 532 A.2d 983, 989 Del. Ch. 1987.) Although the corporation in *David* maintained all necessary formalities, including paying annual fees, the sole Shareholder had used the corporation as a vehicle for committing a fraud upon consumers. Accordingly, the Court pierced the corporate veil and awarded a personal judgment against the corporation's sole Shareholder.

Additional cases also indicate that Delaware courts will not pierce the corporate veil unless "fraud or something like it" is present, regardless of corporate formalities. *See e.g. Mobil Oil Corp.* v. *Linear Films, Inc., 718* F.Supp. 260, 268 (D. Del. 1989). Recent cases suggest that Delaware courts may become more willing to pierce the corporate veil based on a traditional alter ego approach. Under this approach, corporations that serve solely as an alter ego for their owners may have their veils pierced. Corporate formalities play a significant role under an alter ego approach, and may have increasing importance in Delaware courts' treatment of corporations. Despite some uncertainty, Delaware courts still appear more hesitant to pierce the corporate veil than do other courts. And yet, even with its business friendly reputation some commentators have their reservations.

> "The days of Delaware as a state where it was exceptionally difficult to pierce the corporate veil may be numbered." Peter B. Oh, Veil Piercing, at fn. 177 (2010). Professor Oh noted: "From 1986 up to and including 2006, 38.46% of veil-piercing claims under Delaware law prevail."

Which is all the more reason to follow the formalities.

## Florida Cases

Florida courts have been resistant to pierce corporate veils, but they generally follow the approaches taken by other jurisdictions regarding determining whether a corporation is an individual's alter ego. Like Delaware, Florida has refused to pierce the corporate veil or otherwise disregard the corporate existence unless the plaintiff shows that corporation was used to mislead creditors or perpetrate a fraud. In cases involving personal injuries rather than contractual relationships, Florida courts appear to apply the same standard. The result of the Florida approach is that litigants are less likely to pierce the corporate veil and obtain personal judgments against Shareholders.

*Dania Jai-Alai Palace, Inc.* v. *Sykes* is one of the leading Florida cases involving a failed attempt to pierce the corporate veil. 450 S.2d 1114 (Fla. 1984). *Dania* involved a woman who was injured by a subsidiary of the corporation she sought to pierce. The subsidiary conducted valet parking services that allowed access to the parent's business. In determining whether the injured woman could recover against the parent corporation, the Florida Supreme Court restated the two requirements for piercing a corporate veil in Florida: (i) the Shareholders must have improperly used the corporate fiction; and (ii) the Shareholders used the corporate fiction to mislead creditors or perpetrate a fraud. *Id.* at 1118. The Florida Supreme Court found that the parent corporation and its subsidiary were financially independent businesses capable of meeting their obligations and that the subsidiary was not operated to perpetrate a fraud. Accordingly, the court refused to pierce the corporate veil.

In the case of *Ocala Breeders' Sales Co.* v. *Hialeah, Inc.,* a Florida Court of Appeals considered whether to pierce the veil of a subsidiary to enter judgment against a parent corporation. 735 So.2d 542 (Fla. App. 2000). The subsidiary corporation was wholly-owned by the parent corporation, never had its own bank account, and was never adequately capitalized. The subsidiary entered into a lease agreement and incurred numerous obligations, which it failed to fulfill. The plaintiff in the case sought to hold the parent corporation liable for the subsidiary's obligations. In this case, the court found that, not only was the subsidiary corporation the alter ego of the parent, but also that the subsidiary was organized to perpetrate a fraud upon its creditors. Accordingly, the court pierced the subsidiary's corporate veil and attached liability to the parent.

In the case of *American Clearing, Inc. v. Brokerage Computer Systems, Inc.*, 666 F. Supp. 2d 1299, 1308 (M.D. Fla. 2009) the court pierced the corporate veil by finding that a siphoning off of funds was an abuse of the corporate form.

While it is clear that Florida courts will not pierce the corporate veil in the absence of some form of fraud, it remains uncertain which specific factors Florida courts will use to find that a corporation is merely an alter ego. *Ocala* and some commenters suggest that under-capitalization may be the primary factor indicating an alter ego, but, as in all jurisdictions, all corporate formalities should be maintained to protect Shareholders from potential personal liability.

## Georgia Cases

Georgia courts have been hesitant to pierce the corporate veil. They have required plaintiffs to show that the corporation and its parent or controlling shareholder had a unity of interest and that maintaining the corporate fiction would perpetrate fraud or injustice. While these requirements are not atypical, Georgia courts have applied a higher burden of proof for plaintiffs who seek to pierce the veil of a Georgia corporation. Cases in which the Georgia courts have applied their approach illustrate their hesitancy to pierce the corporate veil.

In the leading case of *Anderson* v. *Chatham,* 379 S.E.2d 793 (Ga. App. 1989), the plaintiff was a disgruntled former employee seeking to recover wages owed to him. Through the course of the trial, the sole shareholder of the involved corporations armed the plaintiff with the tools required to pierce the corporate veil. At trial, the defendant employer admitted that "he treated all of the [corporations'] assets as his own because he owned all of the stock in both corporations." *Id.* at 796. "His testimony was replete with other examples of his intermingling of business and personal actions and transactions, including admission that he paid certain personal expenditures from corporate accounts because 'it's just a one man operation.'" *Id.* at 797. The Georgia Court of Appeals agreed with the jury, providing that, "the evidence of Anderson's disregard of the separateness of the legal business entities by a commingling and confusion of properties, records, control, etc. was sufficient to permit the jury to pierce the corporate veils." As an example of veil piercing in a contractual relationship, *Anderson* exemplifies Georgia's willingness to look through the corporate fiction in cases of clear disregard of the corporate form.

While *Anderson* involved a defendant who clearly disregarded the corporate form, it is a rare example of a case in which Georgia courts have been willing to pierce the corporate veil. Generally, Georgia courts agree that "great caution should be exercised by the court" in disregarding the corporate form. *Amason* v. *Whitehead,* 367 S.E.2d 107, 108 (Ga. App. 1988) (quoting *Farmers Warehouse* v. *Collins,* 137 S.E.2d 619 (Ga. 1964». *Amason* discussed the burden facing plaintiffs who seek to pierce the corporate veil. A plaintiff must provide evidence of fraud and abuse of the corporate form; that "the shareholders disregarded the corporate entity and made it a mere instrumentality for the transaction of their own affairs; [and,] that there is such unity of interest and ownership that the separate personalities of the corporation and the owners no longer exist." *Id.* "[I]n order to disregard the corporate entity because a corporation is a mere alter ego or business conduit of a person, [the plaintiff must show that it was] used as a subterfuge so that to observe it would work an injustice." *Id.* at 108. In *Amason,* the plaintiff was a former employee seeking to collect payment for masonry services. He was unable to provide sufficient evidence of fraud or abuse of the corporate form. *Id.* at 109.

*Brown* v. *Rentz,* 441 S.E.2d 876 (Ga. App. 1994), provides another example of Georgia courts' approach to veil piercing. The Browns purchased a home from Lonnie and Linda Rentz. Lonnie was a shareholder, director, and officer in Rentz Builders, Inc., the builder of the home. His wife, Linda, was the corporation's secretary and the real estate agent that sold the home to the Browns. After the Browns moved into the home, they discovered structural problems and sought recovery from the builder, realty company, and Lonnie and Linda Rentz. The court provided that,

> [t]o pierce the corporate veil, there must be abuse of the corporate form. Sole ownership of a corporation by one person or another corporation is not a factor, ... and neither is the fact that the sole owner uses and controls it to promote his ends. The law intervenes when the separate personalities of the corporation and its owner no longer exist.

*Id.* at 877-78. Although invoices and other documents were addressed to Linda or Lonnie personally, there was not sufficient evidence of commingling of corporate and private funds or disregard of the corporate form so as to justify piercing the corporate veil. *Id.* at 878.

Georgia courts have been equally hesitant to pierce the corporate veil in both the context of shareholder veil-piercing and the context of parent and subsidiary veil piercing. *Boafo* v. *Hospital Corporation of America, 338* S.E.2d 477 (Ga. App. 1985), involved a patient's claims against a hospital and his attempt to pierce through the hospital's veil to establish liability for the parent corporation. The plaintiff established that the two corporations shared some officers, they jointly purchased the hospital property, the subsidiary was not incorporated in Georgia until after the property was purchased, the subsidiary was wholly-owned by the parent, some officers were paid only by the parent and the hospital administrator was paid by the parent, major accounting and financial functions were performed by the parent, and the subsidiary was insured by an insurer who was another wholly owned subsidiary of the parent. *See id.* at 478. While the subsidiary could purchase inventory from the parent, it was free to, and did, negotiate its own purchasing contracts if it another provider offered better rates. *See id.* The subsidiary was fully capitalized. *See id.* Despite the many ties between the parent and subsidiary, the Court refused to pierce the subsidiary's corporate veil in *Boafo,* because there was "no evidence that [the subsidiary] was a sham, or that it was used to ... justify wrong, protect fraud, defend crime, or any other reason which in equity and good conscience would justify the disregard of ... [the subsidiary as a] separate entity." *Id. at 479.*

In *Worsham v. Provident Companies, Inc.*, 249 F. Supp. 2d 1325, 1340 (N.D. Ga. 2002) the court held that "Georgia recognizes corporate identity as separate from that of its principals or owners, provided that corporate forms are maintained." Although Georgia courts may hesitate to pierce the corporate veil, as shown in *Anderson,* there are cases in which the corporate form will be disregarded. When conducting business in Georgia, it appears that corporate formalities are less important than they are in other jurisdictions. Nevertheless, prudence dictates that corporations comply with corporate formalities to ensure limited liability for shareholders and parent corporations.

**Illinois Cases**

Illinois courts have applied a two-part analysis to determine whether to pierce the corporate veil. For an Illinois court to pierce the corporate veil, the plaintiff must demonstrate (i) that there is such unity of interest and ownership that the separate personalities of the corporation and the individual no longer exist and (ii) circumstances which exist such that adherence to the fiction of a separate corporate existence would sanction a fraud, promote injustice, or promote inequitable consequences. *See e.g. People ex rel. Scott* v. *Pin tozzi,* 277 N.E.2d 844, 851-52 (Ill. 1971). To show the requisite unity of interest, a plaintiff may refer to the corporation's failure to obey corporate formalities. Cases in which the corporate veil has been pierced are illustrative.

In *People* v. *V & M Industries,* an Illinois appellate court decided that the state of Illinois sufficiently demonstrated a unity of interest and injustice so as to justify piercing the corporate veil. 700 N.E.2d 746 (Ill. App. 1998). V & M Industries's corporate identity was dissolved shortly after a tire fire occurred on its property. The individual who had controlled V & M Industries also controlled several other corporations and had conducted business on behalf of each of the many entities. In the process of doing so, the individual failed to sufficiently distinguish between the entities and deposited money from some entities into the accounts of others. After the tire fire, the individual engaged in a series of transactions that resulted in his personal ownership of V & M Industries' real estate that had not been affected by the fire. The court found each of the following factors present in *V & M Industries,* justifying it to pierce the corporate veil:

1. Inadequate capitalization;
2. Failure to issue stock;
3. Failure to observe corporate formalities;
4. Payment of dividends;
5. Insolvency of the debtor corporation;
6. Corporate officers or directors did not perform their functions;
7. Corporate records were not maintained; and
8. The corporation was a mere facade for the operation of dominant stockholders.

If the court refused to pierce the corporate veil, the state would not be able to recover damages for the environmental harm caused by the tire fire. In piercing the corporate veil, the court applied personal liability to the individual for such harm.

A more restrictive and typical Illinois case is *Cosgrove Distributors, Inc. v. Haff*, 343 Ill. App. 3d 426, 429, 278 Ill. Dec. 292, 798 N.E.2d 139, 141 (3d Dist. 2003) "Courts are reluctant to pierce the corporate veil. Therefore a party seeking to pierce the veil must make a substantial showing that the corporation is really a dummy or sham for another dominating entity." Cosgrove further held that: "For a court to pierce the corporate veil and find the shareholders liable for the corporations obligations, two conditions must be met: (1) a unity of interest and ownership that causes the separate personalities of the corporation and the individual to no longer exist; and (2) the presence of circumstances under adherence to the fiction of a separate corporate existence would sanction a fraud, promote injustice or promote inequitable consequences." See also the case of *International Financial Services Corp. v. Chromas Technologies Canada, Inc.*, 356 F.3d 731, 736 (7th Cir. 2004) "Under the law of Illinois, a party seeking to disregard the corporate entity because the targeted corporation is merely the alter ego of the dominating personality 'must show that (1) there is such a unity of interest and ownership that the separate personalities of the corporation and the individual no longer exist; and (2) circumstances are such that adhering to the fiction of a separate corporate existence would promote injustice or inequity."

Illinois is generally hesitant to pierce corporate veils, but cases revealing misuse of corporations that results in injustice or inequitable consequences may provide grounds for the courts to pierce the corporate veil. Corporate Directors, Officers, and Shareholders may protect themselves from personal liability by ensuring that the corporation follows corporate formalities and by treating the corporation as a distinct legal entity with its own rights and obligations.

## Massachusetts Cases

While some jurisdictions have only recently developed their jurisprudence regarding veil-piercing, others have generally followed precedent long-ago established. Massachusetts has had few recent cases ascend to the level of the Commonwealth's highest court, the Supreme Judicial Court. Instead, most cases of veil piercing in Massachusetts rely on the principles established in *Hanson* v. *Bradley,* 10 N.E.2d 259 (Mass. 1937). *Hanson* arose from an attempt to restore and operate the Copley Square Hotel in Boston. *See id.* at 260. The corporation involved in the venture became heavily indebted to two shareholders, who were eventually given a mortgage on the hotel property. *See id.* at 261-62. When the two shareholders realized that the venture would not succeed, they created a new corporation, foreclosed on the mortgage, and leased the Hotel to the new corporation. *See id.* at 262. The plaintiff was an employee of the failed corporation who sought to pierce the corporation's veil to collect unpaid salary from the two shareholders. *See id.*

In considering whether to pierce the corporate veil of the failed corporation, the Court considered the relationship between the former employee and the corporation and what he knew about the corporation when he contracted to perform services. *See id.* at 264. The plaintiff in *Hanson* knew that the corporation was worthless and that his employment contract was of no value unless the corporation could borrow money. *See id.* "He must have known that lenders have a habit of demanding security." *Id.* Accordingly, the court found that no fraud had been committed and that the plaintiff was not entitled to pierce the corporate veil to collect his salary from the shareholders. *See id.* Essentially, *Hanson* provided that one who deals with a corporation in Massachusetts as a contract creditor is under a duty to investigate the financing of the corporation and assume that some of the lenders and secured credit-holders may be stockholders.

In addition to limiting the remedies available to contract creditors, *Hanson* provided the basic framework for Massachusetts' veil-piercing jurisprudence. The Court provided that, "the right and the duty of courts to look beyond the corporate forms are exercised only for the defeat of fraud or wrong, or the remedying of injustice." *Id.* Under *Hanson,* to pierce the corporate veil in Massachusetts, the plaintiff must show (i) domination or control by a shareholder, and (ii) that the corporation was used in an unjust or fraudulent manner, which is (iii) the proximate cause of damage to the plaintiff.

*My Bread Baking Co.* v. *Cumberland Farms, Inc.,* 233 N.E.2d 748 (Mass. 1968), expanded upon Massachusetts' veil-piercing jurisprudence in the realm of inter-corporate relations. Involving claims arising from common ownership of corporations, *My Bread* provided that common ownership and common management, standing alone, will not give rise to liability on the part of one corporation for the acts of another corporation or its employees. *See id.* at 752. A plaintiff seeking to pierce the corporate veil must provide evidence of agency. *See id.* Veil piercing is possible, however, when (i) shareholders or officers of one corporation control the activities of another and (ii) there is some fraudulent or injurious consequence of the intercorporate relationship. *See id.* Veil piercing is also possible when there is "a confused intermingling of activity of two or more corporations engaged in a common enterprise with substantial disregard of the separate nature of the corporate entities, or serious ambiguity about the manner and capacity in which the various corporations and their respective representatives are acting." *Id.*

For corporations engaging in business in Massachusetts, *My Bread* warned that,

> [w]here there is common control of a group of separate corporations engaged in a single enterprise, failure (a) to make clear which corporation is taking action in a particular situation and the nature and extent of that action, or (b) to observe with care the formal barriers between the corporations with a proper segregation of their separate businesses ... records, and finances, may warrant some disregard of the separate entitles in rare particular situations in order to prevent gross inequity.

*Id.* As acknowledged by *My Bread,* "Massachusetts has been somewhat more 'strict' than other jurisdictions in respecting the separate entities of different corporations." *Id.* For a recent case supporting the My Bread decision see *Motorsport Engineering, Inc. v. Maserati, S.p.A.*, 183 F. Supp. 2d 209,216 (D. Mass. 2001), aff'd, 316 F.3d 26(1st Cir. 2002). Federal courts have applied the Commonwealth's hesitance to pierce the corporate veil. *See e.g. in re Cambridge Biotech Corporation,* 186 F.3d 1356, 1376 (Fed. Cir. 1999) (providing that "Massachusetts law is clear that the corporate veil should only rarely be pierced to prevent "gross inequity"); *Dale* v. *H.B. Smith Company, Inc., 910* F.Supp. 14 (D. Mass. 1995) (providing that, "[I]n order for a court to disregard separate corporate entities, a plaintiff must meet a very high standard.") However, it appears that Massachusetts may be willing to stretch its veil-piercing jurisprudence if overwhelming policy concerns justify doing so. *See Commw.* v. *Phillip Morris Inc.,* 1998 WL 1181992 (Mass. Super. Mar. 20, 1998) (mem.).

While the general approach taken by Massachusetts courts limits veil piercing to extreme circumstances, veil piercing remains an equitable remedy. Accordingly, courts are free to consider various factors in determining whether maintaining the corporate veil will promote injustice. Corporations engaging in business in Massachusetts should be aware of the risk that their actions may lead to personal liability for shareholders. However, the risk involved is less than that involved in conducting business in many other jurisdictions.

## Minnesota Cases

Minnesota courts have consistently applied a two-pronged approach to veil-piercing, first described in *Victoria Elevator Company of Minneapolis* v. *Meriden Grain Co., Inc.,* 283 N.W.2d 509 (Minn. 1979). To pierce the corporate veil, the plaintiff must establish (i) that the corporation was the mere instrumentality of a controlling shareholder or parent corporation, and (ii) that maintaining the corporate form will result in injustice or fundamental unfairness. *Id.* at 512. In determining whether the corporation was a mere instrumentality, Minnesota courts consider the following eight factors:

1. Insufficient capitalization for purposes of corporate undertakings;
2. Failure to observe corporate formalities;
3. Nonpayment of dividends;
4. Insolvency of debtor corporation at time of transaction in question;
5. Siphoning of funds by dominant shareholder;
6. Nonfunctioning of other officers and directors;

7. Absence of corporate records; and

8. Existence of corporation as merely a facade for individual dealings.

*See id.* While courts consider the foregoing factors, courts apply the factors on an equitable basis, making it unclear how many of the factors must be met for a corporation to be considered a mere instrumentality. However, it is clear that meeting the first prong will not require the corporate veil to be pierced; the second prong also must be satisfied.

Cases arising since *Victoria Elevator* have applied its two-prong test and have provided interpretation of the factors involved in meeting the first prong of the test. *Almac, Inc.* v. *JRH Development, Inc.,* 391 N.W.2d 919 (Minn. App. 1986), provided perhaps the most thorough analysis of such factors. Among other things, the plaintiff in *Almac* alleged that (i) the corporate defendant was undercapitalized, (ii) it had ignored corporate formalities, and, (iii) it did not pay dividends. *See id.* At 922-23. While the corporate defendant was insolvent at the time of the trial, the Court considered that fact irrelevant, because "any business which fails can probably be said to have been undercapitalized." *Id.* At 923. Because "the corporation's "total equity kept pace with corporate liabilities until the drastic losses started," the corporation was not undercapitalized under the *Victoria Elevators* standard. *See id.* In considering the lack of corporate formalities, the Court focused on the fact that the corporation was closely held, Minnesota's flexibility in corporate meeting and record requirements, and precedent indicating that directors of closely-held corporations may be passive. *See id.* Furthermore, the *Almac* Court found that the failure to pay dividends did not indicate that the corporation was a mere instrumentality, because funds were retained in the corporation as operating capital. *See id.* The Court concluded that the plaintiff failed to satisfy not only the first prong of the *Victoria Elevator* test, but also the second prong, because "[t]he corporation was formed for bona fide purposes and fulfilled those purposes while it existed." *Id.*

The cases applying the test established in *Victoria Elevator* have continued Minnesota's hesitance to pierce the corporate veil. However, unlike some other jurisdictions, Minnesota has specifically provided that fraud is not an element necessary to pierce the corporate veil. *See Victoria Elevator Company of Minneapolis,* 283 N.W.2d at 512. This indicates that Minnesota may pierce the corporate veil when other jurisdictions would refuse to do so. As in all jurisdictions, veil-piercing in Minnesota is an equitable remedy that is subject to the discretion of the courts. However, Minnesota has provided guidance to corporations by consistently applying the factors that are to be considered and the elements needed to pierce the corporate veil. Accordingly, Minnesota allows corporations security that other jurisdictions with more flexible veil-piercing doctrines fail to provide.

## Nevada Cases

As a state that provides numerous benefits to corporations, such as low maintenance costs, limited taxation, privacy, and management flexibility, Nevada also protects corporations by applying a rigid approach to piercing the corporate veil. As does Delaware, Nevada requires a demonstration of injustice or fraud before a corporate veil may be pierced. However, Nevada also clearly applies its alter ego doctrine to determine whether veil piercing is appropriate.

In *Lorenz* v. *Beltio, Ltd.,* the Nevada Supreme Court applied its alter ego doctrine to pierce Beltio, Ltd.'s corporate veil and create personal liability for the corporation's obligations. 963 P.2d 488 (Nev. 1998). For a corporate veil to be pierced in Nevada, (i) the corporation must be influenced and governed by the person asserted to be its alter ego, (ii) there must be such unity of interest and ownership that one is inseparable from the other, and (iii) the facts must be such that adherence to the fiction of separate entity would, under the circumstances, sanction a fraud or promote injustice. *Id.* at 496 (citing *Ecklund* v. *Nev. Wholesale Lumber Co.,* 562 P.2d 479, 479-80 Nev. 1977.) The corporation's sole Shareholders were also its Directors and Officers, and they conducted the necessary meetings and maintained corporate records. Nevertheless, the court found that the corporation "had no apparent independent business operation and existed solely for the purpose of conducting the personal business of' the Shareholders." *Id.* at 496-497. The court focused on the facts that the Shareholders had commingled corporate and personal funds and had failed to open a separate bank account for the corporation. Additionally, payments to the corporation had been made to the Shareholders personally, and the corporation was undercapitalized. In deciding to pierce the corporate veil in *Lorenz,* the Nevada Supreme Court indicated the many factors it considers in applying its alter ego doctrine.

If undercapitalization is the claim it must be conclusively shown for the corporate veil to be pierced. As stated in the case *North Arlington Medical Building Inc. v. Sanchez Construction Company*, *471 Pzd at 244*:

> "Undercapitalization, where it is clearly shown, is an important factor in determining whether the doctrine of alter ego should be applied. However, in the absence of fraud or injustice to the aggrieved party, it is not an absolute ground for disregarding a corporate entity. In any event it is incumbent upon the one seeking to pierce the corporate veil, to show by a preponderance of the evidence, that the financial setup of the corporation is only a sham and caused an injustice." *Carlesimo v. Schwebel, 197 P.2d 167 (Cal.App. 1948); Arnold v. Phillips, 117 F.2d 497 (CA 5 Tex. 1941); Hanson v. Bradley, 10 N.E.2d 259 (Mass. 1937);* cf: *Tropic Builders Ltd. v. Naval Ammunition Depot, 402 P.2d 440 (Hawaii 1965).*

While the Nevada alter ego doctrine expressly considers corporate formalities, it also limits creditors' ability to pierce the corporate veil by requiring fraud or injustice. The aforementioned case of *Eckland v. Nevada Wholesale Lumber Co.* 562 Pzd 479 (Nev. 1977) discussed the level of fraud required to pierce the veil:

> "A case of injustice was involved in *Carson Meadows, Inc. v. Pease*, 91 Nev. 187, 533 P.2d 458 (1975). In that case, this court held the president and director of a corporation liable in damages to investors he had induced to loan money to the corporation by misrepresenting the corporation as financially sound. The record indicated that the defendant had wholly controlled the corporation and, while not the sole stockholder, had used it and its assets for whatever purposes he wished. Not only were none of the corporate formalities observed, but Goldbeck commingled corporate funds with his own. He treated some corporate assets as his own and manipulated them to suit himself.

He appears to have negotiated all of the corporate business, and truly may be said to have used the corporate shell as a conduit for his individual enterprise." *Id. At 191, 533 P.2d at 421.* No such showing supports the trial courts decision in the instant case.

This court has rejected the alter ego theory in other, less extreme fact situations. *See Plotkin v. National Lead Co., 87 Nev. 51,482 P.2d 323 (1971); North Arlington Medical Building., Inc. v. Sanchez Constr. Co., 86 Nev. 515, 471 P.2d 240 (1970); Baer v. Amos J. Walker, Inc., 85 Nev. 219, 452 P.2d 916 (1969); O'Connell v. Cox, 78 Nev. 40, 368 P.2d 761 (1962); and Nevada Tax Comm'n v. Hicks, 73 Nev. 115, 310 P.2d 852 (1957).*

The instant case is allied with those cases in which the corporate entity was upheld. Respondent failed to meet its burden of establishing the three required elements of the alter ego doctrine." (*562 Pzd at 481.*)

In 2001, the Nevada legislature incorporated the three part test into its code at NRS 78.747: "Liability of stockholder, director or officer for debt or liability of corporation:"

1. Except as otherwise provided by specific statute, no stockholder, director or officer of a corporation is individually liable for a debt or liability of the corporation, unless the stockholder, director or officer acts as the alter ego of the corporation.

2. A stockholder, director or officer acts as the alter ego of a corporation if:

   a. The corporation is influenced and governed by the stockholder, director or officer;

   b. There is such unity of interest and ownership that the corporation and the stockholder, director or officer are inseparable from each other; and

   c. Adherence to the corporate fiction of a separate entity would sanction fraud or promote a manifest injustice.

3. The question of whether a stockholder, director or officer acts as the alter ego of a corporation must be determined by the court as a matter of law.

With this legislation Nevada has clearly stated its restrictive approach to veil piercing. Still, a strict approach to following corporate formalities is always in order.

## New York Cases

The contemporary approach New York courts take to piercing the corporate veil is based on an amalgamation of earlier New York case law and federal courts' interpretation of New York law. The result is an approach that is changing from being extremely conservative to being more lenient. While New York courts traditionally required that the corporation commit some wrong or fraud before its veil could be pierced, recent federal decisions purporting to apply New York state law do not requires such a wrong and allow judges great discretion in veil piercing.

The traditional conservative New York approach to veil piercing was established by three cases decided between 1926 and 1966, all of which limited creditors' ability to pierce the corporate veil to cases in which the corporation engaged in some form of wrongdoing. *See Walkovszky* v. *Carlton,* 223 N.E.2d 6 (1966); *Bartle* v. *Home Owners Cooperative, 127* N.E.2d 832 (1955); *Berkey* v. *Third Ave. Ry. Co.,* 155 N.E. 58 (1926). The three landmark cases used differing language and tests to provide essentially that the corporate veil would not be pierced unless the corporation engaged in fraud, misrepresentation, or illegal acts. Only under such circumstances would public policy concerns justify the courts to disregard the corporate existence and apply personal liability.

Recent cases have also held to the traditional New York approach. *State v. Robin Operating Corp.*, 3 A.D.3d 769, 773 N.Y.S.2d 137, 2004 N.Y. Slip Op. 00305 (3rd Dept. 2004) Failure to show "complete domination of the corporation [that] is the key to piercing the corporate veil" under New York law; *Alpha Bytes Computer Corp. v. Slaton*, 307 A.D.2d 725, 726, 762 N.Y.S.2d 328 (4th Dep't 2003) Determination to pierce the corporate veil is fact-laden and thus is not well suited for resolution by summary judgment, showing of both complete domination and fraud or wrong required, but not shown in the instant case so grant of summary judgment on that point denied; *Vitale v. Steinberg*, 307 A.D.2d 107, 764 N.Y.S.2d 236 (1st Dep't 2003) Requisite self–dealing for finding an abuse sufficient to pierce the corporate veil not found.

New York's rigid traditional approach precludes veil piercing in most cases, but federal cases that claim to apply New York law offer courts and litigants more flexibility in veil piercing. Federal courts consider all corporate formalities as relevant to the determination of whether to pierce the corporate veil. For example, in *Wausau Business Insurance Co.* v. *Turner Construction Co.,* a federal district court provided that

> New York law allows courts to pierce the corporate veil either where a fraud has been committed, *or* where the corporation has been so dominated by an individual or corporate parent that the subsidiary is relegated to the status of a mere shell, instrumentality, or alter ego.

141 F. Supp. 2d 412, 417 (S.D.N.Y. 2001) (citing *Wm. Passalacqua Builders, Inc.* v. *Resnick Developers S; Inc.,* 933 F.2d 131 (2d Cir. 1991) (emphasis added). The *Wausau* court continued to provide the following factors considered when determining if a corporation was a shell, instrumentality, or alter ego:

1. Failure to observe corporate formalities;
2. Under-capitalization;
3. Intermingling of corporate funds;
4. Overlap in Officers, Directors, and personnel between parent and subsidiary corporation;
5. Common office space, address and telephone numbers;
6. The amount of business discretion exercised by the subsidiary corporation;
7. Whether the two companies deal with each other at arm's length;
8. Whether the corporations exist as independent sources of profit;
9. The guarantee of the subsidiary's debts by the parent; and
10. Common use of corporate property.

*Id.* Although the *Wausau* court did not pierce the corporate veil, the *Passalacqua* case, upon which the *Wausau* court relied, pierced a corporate veil without showing that the corporation engaged in fraud or other wrongdoing. These opinions from federal courts provide litigants with potential veil piercing arguments.

The traditional approach taken by New York courts protects shareholders from personal liability unless they use the corporation to commit some wrongful act, but federal courts may have started a new trend in New York veil piercing. This new trend would allow courts to pierce the corporate veil simply because shareholders and management fail to accord the corporation the proper respect as an independent entity.

In fact, while reported New York cases evidence a traditional approach, a recent review of New York cases indicates otherwise. In a 2010 study entitled Veil-Piercing by Peter B. Oh it was found that 42.46% of state court cases pierced the corporate veil and in federal courts it was pierced 56.14% of the time. As a consequence, such rulings encourage Shareholders, Directors and Officers to ensure that the corporation follows all necessary procedures to maintain its separate identity.

**Pennsylvania Cases**

Pennsylvania's approach to piercing the corporate veil is a source of uncertainty. As a preliminary issue, it is important to note that Pennsylvania courts clearly distinguish between veil piercing cases involving a parent/subsidiary relationship and those in which a plaintiff seeks to obtain a personal judgment against a corporation's Director, Officer, or Shareholder.

While Pennsylvania has applied an alter ego doctrine to cases involving personal liability, it has not adopted the common "single entity" approach to cases involving parent/subsidiary veil piercing. *See Miners Inc.* v. *Alpine Equip. Corp.,* 722 A.2d 691(Pa. Super. 1998). Without a clear doctrinal approach to parent/subsidiary veil piercing, Pennsylvania corporations are not provided with guidelines. Even in its application of its alter ego doctrine, Pennsylvania has provided a source for uncertainty.

Many jurisdictions, including Pennsylvania, use a two-part alter ego analysis to determine whether the corporate veil may be pierced and individual Directors, Officer, or Shareholders held personally liable. First, Pennsylvania courts determine whether the corporation is the alter ego of its Directors, Officers or Shareholders. Second, Pennsylvania courts consider the consequences of treating the corporation as a separate legal entity. While other jurisdictions often require a plaintiff to show that maintaining the corporate identity will perpetrate a fraud or injustice or result in inequitable consequences, Pennsylvania courts have somewhat rejected this requirement. In *Village at Camelback Property Owners Association,* v. *Carr,* a Pennsylvania appellate court provided that

> [l]iability for the acts of a corporation may be assessed against the owners thereof wherever equity requires that such be done either to prevent fraud, illegality or injustice or when recognition of the corporate entity would defeat public policy or shield someone from public liability for crime. (citations omitted) Nevertheless, the corporate existence can be disregarded without a specific showing of fraud.

538 A.2d 528, 533 (Pa. Super. 1988). It is now uncertain whether Pennsylvania requires a plaintiff to make allegations regarding the consequences of maintaining the corporate veil. "There appears to be no clear test or well settled rule in Pennsylvania ... as to exactly when the corporate veil can be pierced and when it may not be pierced." *Good* v. *Holstein,* 787 A.2d 426, 430 (Pa. Super. 2001). Nevertheless, Pennsylvania cases all provide that there is a strong presumption in Pennsylvania against piercing the corporate veil. See, e.g., *Shay v. Flight C Helicopter Services, Inc.*, 2003 PA Super 86, 822 A.2d 1, 19 (2003) The doctrine of piercing the corporate veil in Pennsylvania "is imposed cautiously and, in fact, there is a presumption against piercing the corporate veil." If no showing of fraud is required, Directors, Officers and

Shareholders in Pennsylvania are subjected to a higher risk of personal liability than in other jurisdictions, because plaintiffs will be required only to show that the corporation is merely an alter ego.

Although it remains uncertain whether Pennsylvania courts require evidence of fraud or injustice to pierce the corporate veil, Pennsylvania courts have identified factors they will consider in determining whether a corporation is the alter ego of its Directors, Officers or Shareholders. Pennsylvania courts have required a plaintiff to show, among other things, that corporate formalities have not been observed or corporate records kept, that Officers and Directors other than the dominant Shareholder did not function in their official capacities, and that the dominant Shareholder used the assets of the corporation as if they were his or her own. *Carr,* 538 A.2d at 533.

Pennsylvania courts also consider evidence of under-capitalization and a failure to adhere to corporate formalities. *Lumax Indus.* v. *Aultman,* 669 A.2d 893, 895 (Pa. 1995). Due to the uncertainty involved in Pennsylvania's veil piercing case law, corporate Directors, Officers and Shareholders may best protect themselves by ensuring that all corporate formalities are followed and treating the corporation as a distinct legal entity.

While veil piercing creates personal liability arising from the corporation's obligations, corporate Directors and Officers may be personally liable for acts they perform on the corporation's behalf. Pennsylvania may hold Directors and Officers personally liable through its "participation theory."

> Under the participation theory, the court imposes liability on the individual as an actor rather than as an owner. Such liability is not predicated on a finding that the corporation is a sham and a mere alter ego of the individual corporate officer. Instead, liability attaches where the record establishes the individual's participation in the tortious [or wrongful] activity.

*Brindley* v. *Woodland Village Restaurant,* 652 A.2d 865, 868 (Pa. Super. 1995). Under the participation theory, Directors and Officers may be held liable not only for what they do, but also for what they fail to do. *Id.* Accordingly, corporate Directors and Officers in Pennsylvania or engaging in business in Pennsylvania should exercise great caution in the actions they take on the corporation's behalf and in the way they relate to the corporation.

While Pennsylvania does not apply unique approaches or approaches that place corporate actors at great risk for personal liability, it does provide uncertainty. Uncertainty in business, as in law, requires extra efforts to minimize risks. To minimize the risks of personal liability in Pennsylvania, corporate actors must comply with all corporate formalities and use care when acting on the corporation's behalf.

## Texas Cases

Texas law regarding corporate veil piercing has undergone changes in the courts and through legislative responses to court action. The landmark case that provided a flexible veil piercing approach was subsequently limited by legislation. *Compare Castleberry* v. *Branscum,* 721 S.W.2d 270 (Tex. *1986); with* Tex. Bus. Corp. Act Ann. art. 2.21 (available in WL TX-ST database). The result is a patchwork of precedent and statutory law that defines when a corporate veil may be pierced.

Although many contours of Texas law remain unexplored, generally, Texas courts will not disregard the corporate identity unless

1. The corporate fiction is used as a means of perpetrating fraud;
2. The corporation is organized and operated as a mere tool or business conduit of another corporation;
3. The corporate fiction is resorted to as a means of evading an existing legal obligation;

4. The corporate fiction is employed to achieve or perpetrate a monopoly;
5. The corporate fiction is used to circumvent a statute; or
6. The corporate fiction is relied upon as a protection of crime or to justify wrong.

*Seminole Pipeline Co.* v. *Broad Leaf Partners, Inc.,* 979 S.W.2d 730, 739 (Tex. App. 1998). "[A ]bsent a showing of wrongdoing on the part of the parent corporation, Texas courts have refused to make the parent liable for its subsidiary's torts." *Id.* In contractual cases, Texas courts also apply the common alter ego theory to determine whether a corporate veil may be pierced. Under Texas's alter ego theory, a corporate veil will not be pierced unless (i) there is such a unity that the separateness of the corporation and its parent/Shareholder(s) has ceased to exist and (ii) adherence to the corporate fiction would promote injustice. *Robbins* v. *Robbins,* 727 S.W.2d 743 (Tex. App. 1987).

While it is clear that the corporate veil will be pierced in cases in which Shareholders' use a corporation to commit actual fraud, it remains uncertain whether constructive fraud will suffice to pierce the corporate veil. Under *Castleberry,* constructive fraud would have sufficed for a finding of alter ego. However, recent cases applying Article 2.21 of the Texas Business Corporations Act have limited the application of alter ego. Such cases have provided that a failure to maintain corporate formalities does not necessarily result in application of the alter ego doctrine. *See Hinkle* v. *Adams,* 74 S.W.3d 189,194 (Tex. App. 2002) (finding that alter ego doctrine did not apply, even though corporation had its charter temporarily revoked after failing to pay its annual franchise taxes when due). A recent case provides some further guidance. In a strong opinion written by Justice Hecht the Texas Supreme Court found in *SSP Partners v. Gladstong Investments (USA) Corp.*, 52 Tex. Sup. Ct. J. 95, 2008 WL 4891733 (Tex. 2008) that the single business enterprise liability theory "is fundamentally inconsistent with the approach taken by the [Texas] Legislature," and that "the single business enterprise liability theory … will not support the imposition of one corporation's obligations on another." Justice Hecht further opined that "Creation of affiliated corporations to limit liability while pursuing common goals lies firmly within the law and is commonplace," and further that "[w]e have never held corporation liable for each other's obligations merely because of centralized control, mutual purposes, and shared finances." For a veil to be pierced, "There must also be evidence of abuse, or as we said in *Castleberry*, injustice and inequity." Accordingly, the formerly lenient standard used by Texas courts may be replaced by a more rigid approach that provides greater protection for Shareholders and corporate management. Nevertheless, corporate actors should use caution to avoid personal liability.

**Utah Cases**

Utah applies a lenient approach to corporate veil piercing that allows creditors and other plaintiffs to pierce a corporate veil with more ease than in other jurisdictions. Under Utah's alter ego doctrine, a court may disregard the corporate fiction if (i) there is such a unity of interest and ownership that the separate personalities of the corporation and the individual no longer exist, but the corporation is, instead, the alter ego of one or a few individuals *and* (ii) if maintained, the corporate fiction would sanction a fraud, promote injustice, or result in an inequity. *Envirotech Corp.* v. *Callahan,* 872 P.2d 487,499 (Utah App. 1994). Utah courts allow creditors to pierce corporate veils through a flexible definition of "injustice" and "inequality."

Utah courts have combined tests regarding corporate formalities with those used to measure injustice, both of which are now based on the following:

1. Under-capitalization of a one-man corporation;

2. Failure to observe corporate formalities;

3. Nonpayment of dividends;

4. Siphoning of corporate funds by the dominant Shareholder;

5. Failures of Directors or Officers to function in their roles;

6. Absence of corporate records;
7. Use of the corporation as a facade for the dominant Shareholder(s), operations; and
8. Use of the corporate property in promoting injustice or fraud.

*Coleman* v. *Coleman,* 743 P.2d 782, 786 (Utah App. 1987). If a sufficient number of these factors are met, a Utah court may find that the corporation is the alter ego of the Shareholder(s) and pierce the corporate veil to find personal liability for the Shareholder(s).

In cases involving a parent and subsidiary corporation, Utah courts have considered whether:

1. The parent corporation owns all or most of the capital stock of the subsidiary;
2. The parent corporation finances the subsidiary;"
3. "[T]he subsidiary has grossly inadequate capital;
4. The parent corporation pays the salaries and other expenses or losses of the subsidiary;
5. The directors or executives of the subsidiary do not act independently in the interest of the subsidiary but take their orders from the parent corporation in the latter's interest; and
6. The formal legal requirements of the subsidiary are not observed.

*Salt Lake City Corp.* v. *James Constructors,* 761 P.2d 42, 47 (Utah App. 1988). A footnote in *James Constructors* suggests that under-capitalization may carry special weight in a court's consideration of whether the subsidiary corporation is the parent's alter ego.

Unlike some other states that provide a rigid test for whether the corporate veil may be pierced and require fraud or something like it, Utah emphasizes the equitable nature of their approach and provides individual judges with discretion to determine whether the veil should be pierced based on the facts of each case. While this may allow the courts greater flexibility, it provides businesses with uncertainty. To ensure that a Utah court will not pierce the corporate veil, a corporation should avoid the factors listed above and clearly maintain all corporate formalities.

## Virginia Cases

In *Cheatle v. Rudd's Swimming Pool Supply* (360 SE 828 1987) the Virginia Supreme Court held:

> "that a corporation is a legal entity entirely separate and distinct from the shareholders or members who compose it. This immunity of stockholders is a basic provision of statutory and common law and supports a vital economic policy underlying the whole corporate concept." Ignoring immunity of stockholders, then, was "an extraordinary exception" and could be permitted "only when it becomes necessary to promote justice."

The court quoted the case approvingly in *CF. Trust, Inc. v. First Flight L.P., 266 Va. 3, 10, 580 S.E.2d 806, 809 (2003).*

In the 2010 Veil-Piercing survey by Peter B. Oh, Virginia ranked one of the least successful states for veil piercing cases. Still, prudence requires a following of the corporate formalities.

## Washington Cases

Rather than applying the typical alter ego terminology used to refer to the application of personal liability to Directors, Officers or Shareholders, Washington courts apply such liability through their doctrine of corporate disregard. The doctrine of corporate disregard applies to establish personal liability when (i) the corporate form was intentionally used to violate or evade a duty, and (ii) disregard is necessary to prevent unjustified loss to the injured party.

> With regard to the first element, the court must find an abuse of the corporate form. (citation omitted) [S]uch an abuse generally involves fraud, misrepresentation, or some form of manipulation of the corporation to the stockholder's benefit and creditor's detriment. With respect to the second element, wrongful corporate activities must actually harm the party

> seeking relief so that disregard is necessary. Intentional misconduct must be the cause of the harm that is avoided by disregard.

*Norhawk Investments, Inc.* v. *Subway Sandwich Shops, Inc.,* 811 P .2d 221,222-23 (Wash. App. 1991). In addition, Washington courts often require evidence that the defendant Director, Officer, or Shareholder dominated or controlled the corporation. The doctrine of corporate disregard establishes a high evidentiary burden for plaintiffs who seek to pierce a corporate veil in Washington and substantially protects corporate actors from personal liability. In *Norhawk Investments, Inc.,* a Washington appellate court refused to pierce the corporate veil of a franchisee to hold the franchisor liable for the franchisee's breach of a commercial lease. Essentially, a Subway franchisee failed to make its rent payments and abandoned the property. The landlord sought to collect money owed under the rental agreement. When the landlord could not collect the money from the franchisee, it sought to collect from the franchisor. To allow collection against the franchisor, Doctor's Associates, Inc., the court would have had to pierce the corporate veil of the franchisor's subsidiary, Subway Sandwich Shops, Inc.

The landlord in *Norhawk Investments, Inc.,* claimed that Subway Sandwich Shops, Inc.'s corporate veil should be pierced, because Subway Sandwich Shops, Inc., was undercapitalized and the landlord suffered harm because of its under-capitalization. While the landlord conceded that no fraud was committed, it claimed that deliberate under-capitalization is an abuse of the corporate form. The court rejected the landlord's argument, providing that "the separate existence of a corporation should not be disregarded solely because its assets are not sufficient to discharge its obligations." *Norhawk,* 811 P.2d at 223. Although the landlord was denied recovery when the court maintained the corporate veil of Subway Sandwich Shops, Inc., the court stated that, "harm alone does not create corporate misconduct." *Id.* The court found that Subway Sandwich Shops, Inc., was operated to limit its parent's liability, limit tax liability, and provide control of leased properties. The court approved of such purposes for a corporation and maintained the corporate veil.

In *Howard* v. *Pidgeon,* a Washington appellate court pierced a construction company's corporate veil to impose personal liability for shareholders who caused the corporation to divert corporate opportunities away from the corporation and breach a promissory note. 1999 Wash. App. LEXIS 670 (unpublished opinion). The plaintiffs and the defendants in *Howard* jointly formed a corporation to develop the defendants' existing construction business. After the relationship soured, the corporation signed a promissory note to purchase the plaintiffs' shares of stock. The corporation became unable to satisfy the promissory note. In deciding to pierce the corporate veil and apply personal liability to the defendants for the amount of the promissory note, the court found that the defendants wasted and diverted funds from the corporation, misused corporate funds, and diverted business opportunities and revenues from the corporation to other businesses they controlled. The defendants' actions caused the corporation to be unable to meet its obligations to the plaintiffs. To prevent the plaintiffs from suffering harm and to enforce the corporation's contractual duties, the court pierced the corporate veil and imposed personal liability upon the defendants for the amount owed to the plaintiffs under the promissory note.

While Washington courts may be slightly more hesitant than many other state courts to pierce the corporate veil, blatant misuse of corporations will justify courts to disregard their existence and impose personal liability or liability for a parent corporation. To avoid such liability, parent corporations, Directors, Officers and Shareholders should refrain from using corporations to avoid their duties to others, including their duties to creditors. Maintaining corporate formalities and treating the corporation like a distinct legal entity will reduce the potential for misusing a corporation.

### Wyoming Cases

Wyoming has only recently begun to form its law regarding veil piercing, and, accordingly, does not provide much guidance for corporations that desire to retain limited liability. In addition to having a dearth of case law, Wyoming has treated veil piercing as a fact-specific inquiry and has refused to provide clear guidelines for future decisions. Nevertheless, Wyoming precedent provides that a corporate veil may be pierced if evidence shows that (i) the corporation is influenced and governed by a person so that there is (ii) such a unity of interest and ownership that the individuality, or separateness, of such person and corporation has ceased, and (iii) the court's adherence to the fiction of the corporation's separate existence would sanction a fraud or promote injustice. *Miles* v. *CEC Homes,* 753 P.2d 1021, 1023 (Wyo. 1988) (citing *AMFAC Mechanical Supply Co.* v. *Federer, 645* P.2d 73, 77 (Wyo. 1982.) The approach adopted by Wyoming courts resembles that applied in many other states, but Wyoming carefully considers the facts of each case before piercing a corporate veil. This provides uncertainty and requires corporations to use caution to avoid losing limited liability. In *Panamerican Mineral Services* v. *KLS Environmental Resources,* the Wyoming Supreme Court indicated factors that Wyoming courts may consider in deciding whether to pierce the corporate veil. 916 P .2d 986 (Wyo. 1996). While *Panamerican* indicated that evidence of fraud alone may be enough for a Wyoming court to pierce the corporate veil, it also reveals the following considerations:

1. Commingling of funds and other assets, failure to segregate funds of the separate entities, and the unauthorized diversion of corporate funds or assets to other than corporate uses;

2. Treatment by an individual of the assets of the corporation as his own;

3. Failure to obtain authority to issue or subscribe to stock;

4. Holding out by an individual that he is personally liable for the debts of the corporation;

5. Failure to maintain minutes or adequate corporate records and the contusion of the

records of the separate entities;

6. Identical equitable ownership in two entities;

7. Identification of the equitable owners thereof with the domination and control of two entities;

8. Identification of the directors and officers of two entities in the responsible supervision and management;

9. Absence of corporate assets and a failure to adequately capitalize the corporation;

10. Use of a corporation as a mere shell, instrumentality or conduit for a single venture or the business of an individual or another corporation;

11. Concealment and misrepresentation of the identity of the responsible ownership, management and financial interest or concealment of personal business activities;

12. Disregard of legal formalities and the failure to maintain arm's length relationships among related entities;

13. Use of the corporate entity to procure labor, services or merchandise for another person or entity;

14. Diversion of assets from a corporation by or to a stockholder or other person or entity, to the detriment of creditors, or the manipulation of assets and liabilities between entities so as to concentrate the assets in one and the liabilities in another;

15. Contracting with another with intent to avoid performance by use of a corporation as a subterfuge of illegal transactions; and,

16. Formation and use of a corporation to transfer to it the existing liability of another person or entity.

*Id.* at 990. While the laundry list of considerations may help to direct corporations away from certain practices, it does not provide absolute limitations on corporations. Many corporations that exhibit some of the characteristics provided above may be able to retain their corporate veil, but others may not. Because Wyoming approaches each case of veil piercing through its unique circumstances, the list of considerations is at best advisory.

A recent case discussing whether Wyoming should apply its veil piercing jurisprudence to limited liability companies provides further insight to the approach Wyoming courts take to corporate veil piercing. In *Kaycee Land & Livestock v. Flahive,* the Wyoming Supreme Court provided that Wyoming courts apply a fact-driven inquiry to determine whether the corporate veil may be pierced. 46 P.3d 323 (Wyo. 2002). The plaintiff in *Kaycee* had asked the court to pronounce that corporate veil piercing standards apply to limited liability companies. The court refused to make such a broad pronouncement. However, it did provide that "no reason exists in law or equity for treating an LLC differently than a corporation is treated when considering whether to disregard the legal entity." *Id.* at 329.

In the later case of *Gasstop Two, LLC v. Seatwo, LLC* the court cited the *Whynott LLC* treatise:

> "The LLC veil piercing factors used from the corporate arena can be reduced to four categories: 1. Fraud; 2. Inadequate capitalization; 3. Failure to observe company formalities; and 4. Intermingling the business and finances of the company and the member to such an extent that there is not distinction between them."

The court then went on to state that "... undercapitalization by itself is not grounds to pierce an LLC veil. Where all corporate formalities were followed, undercapitalization was not the only pertinent factor to be considered in piercing the corporate veil. *Amfac Mechanical Supply Co. v. Federe, 645 P.2d 73, 82 (Wyo. 1982) See 225 P.3d at 1078.*

And in conclusion, after reviewing all the facts of the case, the court held that the defendants:

> "... operated SEATWO in substantial conformity with the rules set forth to operate an LLC. They kept all personal and business assets separate. They filed the appropriate paperwork with the Secretary of State, and operated as a prudent LLC. This Court finds no evidence to pierce the LLC veil." *225 P.3d at 1079.*

By making veil piercing available against limited liability companies, the Wyoming Supreme Court continued its treatment of veil piercing as a fact-specific remedy that is decided through principles of fairness.

## Conclusion

As the foregoing pages reveal, states apply similar approaches to veil piercing, but with differing results. In all jurisdictions, courts decide whether to pierce the corporate veil based on the specific circumstances of each case.

Piercing the corporate veil, as we have discussed, is an equitable remedy, which means that courts look to provide fair results in applying established standards. If the standard does not provide a fair result, the courts are free to modify the standard to provide "equity," or fairness, in the case at hand. While we have surveyed the approaches courts in each jurisdiction have taken in the past, courts focus on the facts of each case in determining whether to pierce the corporate veil. Accordingly, it is exceedingly difficult to predict the outcome of future cases, and we expressly disclaim any ability to do so.

Even states that provide the clearest standards may reach surprising results. Additionally, federal courts may misinterpret a state's approach and apply personal liability where a state court would not. At best, understanding a specific jurisdiction's approach to veil piercing will be instructive as to what practices or situations corporations should avoid.

# VII. Concluding Statements

Although jurisdictions may require slightly different elements to justify piercing a corporate veil, the message to corporate Officers, Directors, and Shareholders is the same: To retain the benefits corporations provide, your business must look and act like a corporation. The steps provided above to raising a corporate veil and the corporate formalities required to maintain the veil should protect corporate actors from personal liability in any jurisdiction. In addition, the formalities will help retain tax and other benefits that operating as a corporation provides for businesses. (Please note that the same applies to limited liability companies and limited partnerships.)

Operating or owning a business provides independence and opportunities that cannot be otherwise obtained. Using a corporation for your business may provide additional benefits and make your experience as an entrepreneur more personally, professionally and financially rewarding. As with any business venture, the advice you seek and receive may determine your capabilities in using a corporation. Because each situation is unique, you should consult with legal, tax, and other advisors that are necessary to ensure the stability of your plan and your future. This book can provide you with the foundation for using a corporation, but achieving corporate success is up to you. Good Luck.

# FORMS APPENDIX

**Appendix A:**
**Articles of Incorporation**

**Appendix B:**
**Consent to Serve as Resident Agent**

**Appendix C:**
**Minutes of Organizational Meetings of Shareholders and Directors**

**Appendix D:**
**Directors and Officers Checklist**

**Appendix E:**
**Waiver of Notice and Notice of Special Meeting**

**Appendix F:**
**Minutes of Shareholders Meeting**

**Appendix G:**
**Minutes of Directors Meetings**
**Minutes of Annual Meeting of Board of Directors**

**Appendix H:**
**Minutes of Directors Meeting**
**Written Consent for Action**

# Appendix A: Articles of Incorporation

**ARTICLES OF INCORPORATION**
**OF**

**XYZ, INC.**

ARTICLE I

NAME: The name of the corporation shall be XYZ, INC.

ARTICLE II

PURPOSE: The purpose for which this corporation is organized is the transaction of any or all lawful purposes for which corporations may be incorporated under the laws of the State of Nevada, as they may be amended from time to time.

ARTICLE III

INITIAL BUSINESS: The corporation initially intends to produce corporate books in this state and to operate a book sales business.

Any business

ARTICLE IV

AUTHORIZED CAPITAL: The corporation shall have the authority to issue fifty million (50,000,000) shares of common stock of the par value of one mill ($0.001) per share.

ARTICLE V

STATUTORY AGENT: The name and address of the initial Statutory Agent, a bona fide resident of Nevada for three years is:

Corporate Direct, Inc.
2248 Meridian Blvd., Suite H
Minden, NV 89423

ARTICLE VI

BOARD OF DIRECTORS: The initial Board of Directors shall consist of two (2) Directors. The person(s) who are to serve as Directors until the first annual meetings of the shareholders or until their successors are elected and qualified are:

Jack Smith, 2248 Meridian Blvd., Suite H, Minden, NV, 89423

Jill Jones, 2248 Meridian Blvd., Suite H, Minden, NV, 89423

The Directors are also the incorporators.

______________________________ ______________________________

Jack Smith Jill Jones

DATED THIS _____ day of _____, 20___.

## Appendix B: Consent to Serve as Resident Agent

### CERTIFICATE OF ACCEPTANCE OF APPOINTMENT BY RESIDENT AGENT

IN THE MATTER OF: **(Name of business entity)**

I, **John Smith** for Corporate Direct, Inc., herby state that on **(date)**

I accepted the appointment as resident agent for the above-named business entity.

The street address of the resident agent in this state is as follows:

Corporate Direct, Inc.
2248 Meridian Blvd., Suite H
Minden, NV 89423

Date:

________________________________________________
Authorized Signature of Resident Agent or Resident Agent Company
John Smith, for Corporate Direct, Inc.

# Appendix C: Minutes of Organizational Meetings of Shareholders and Directors

## MINUTES OF THE FIRST MEETING OF SHAREHOLDERS OF XYZ, INC.

Upon proper notice, the first meeting of XYZ, Inc. was held on ____________________, 20___. The meeting was called to order by Jack Smith, the incorporator, and the following shareholders, being a majority of the shareholders of the Corporation, were present:

**Jack Smith**
**Jill Jones**

Jack Smith acted as Secretary of the meeting.

There was presented to the meeting as follows:

1. Copy of Certificate of Incorporation;
2. Copy of the By-Laws of the Corporation;
3. Resignation of the Incorporator;
4. Corporate certificate book; and
5. Corporate certificate ledge.

The Chairman noted that it was in order to consider electing a Board of Directors for the ensuing year. Upon nominations duly made, seconded and unanimously carried, the following persons were elected as Directors of the Corporation, to serve for a period of one year and until such time as their successors are elected and qualify:

**Jack Smith**
**Jill Jones**

Upon motion duly made, seconded and unanimously carried, it was

**RESOLVED**, that the items listed above have been examined by all shareholders, and are all approved and adopted, and that all acts taken and decisions reached as set forth in such documents be, and they hereby are, ratified and approved by the shareholders of the Corporation.

There being no further business to come before the meeting, upon motion duly made, seconded and unanimously carried, it was adjourned.

______________________________
Jack Smith, Secretary

**ORGANIZATIONAL MINUTES OF THE BOARD OF DIRECTORS OF XYZ, INC.**

The organization meeting of the Board of Directors of XYZ, Inc. was held on __________________, 20____.

Jack Smith and Jill Jones, constituting the total members of the initial Board of Directors of the Corporation, and a quorum, were present.

Jill Jones as Secretary of the meeting and Jack Smith acted as Chairman of the meeting.

The Chairman reported that the Articles of Incorporation had been filed with the Secretary of State of the State of _____________. The Secretary was directed to insert a certified copy of the Articles in the minute books as part of these minutes.

The Secretary then submitted to the meeting the seal proposed for use as the Corporation, along with a form of the stock certificate. After reviewing the seal and the stock certificate and upon motion duly made, seconded and unanimously carried it was:

The Secretary submitted to the meeting a seal proposed for use as the corporate seal of the Corporation, along with a form of the stock certificate. After reviewing the seal and the stock certificate, and upon motion duly made, seconded, and unanimously carried, it was:

> **RESOLVED**, that the form of the seal and the stock certificate submitted to this meeting are adopted and approved as the corporate seal and stock certificate of the Corporation. The Secretary of the Corporation is hereby authorized and directed to insert a copy of the stock certificate with these minutes, and to affix an impression of the seal on the margin of these minutes.

The Secretary then presented the proposed Code of Bylaws relating to the regulation of the business and affairs of the Corporation, its shareholders, Directors, and officers. After reviewing the proposed Code of Bylaws and upon motion duly made, seconded, and unanimously carried, it was:

> **RESOLVED,** that the Code of Bylaws presented to this meeting is adopted as the Code of Bylaws of the Corporation, and the Secretary is directed to certify and insert the Code of Bylaws into the minute book (containing the minutes of the proceedings of the Board of Directors and other relevant corporate documents).

The Chairman stated that the next order of business was the election of the officers as specified in the Code of Bylaws. The Chairman called for nominations for officers to serve for one year or until their successors are elected or qualified. After discussion, the following persons were nominated and seconded to the following positions:

| | |
|---|---|
| Jack Smith | President |
| Jill Jones | Secretary |
| Jill Jones | Treasurer |

The Chairman called for further nominations, but none were made. A voice vote was taken and since there was no opposition, the Chairman declared that the nominees are the duly elected officers of the Corporation to serve until the next annual Board meeting, or until their successors are elected and shall qualify.

The Chairman stated that the next order of business was to determine the compensation of the officers. After discussion and upon motion duly made, seconded and unanimously carried, it was:

> **RESOLVED,** that the salary of the corporate officers shall be (________________) or (determined at a later date.)

The Chairman stated that the next order of business was to consider compensation of the Officers. After discussion, upon motion duly made, seconded, and unanimously carried, it was:

> **RESOLVED,** that the Treasurer of the Corporation be authorized and directed to pay all charges and expenses incident to the formation and organization of this Corporation and to reimburse all persons who have made any disbursements for such charges and expenses.

The Chairman stated that the next order of business was to consider the designation of a Registered Agent and registered office of the Corporation in the State of ______________. The Chairman stated that the Articles of Incorporation stated that ________________ is the Registered Agent of the Corporation and the principal place of business is ________________ ________________. Upon motion duly made, seconded, and unanimously carried, it was:

> **RESOLVED,** that ______________________, be and herby is appointed Registered Agent for the Corporation in the State of ______________. The office of the Registered Agent is ______________ __________.

After a discussion and upon motion duly made, seconded and unanimously carried, it was:

> **RESOLVED,** that SUTTON LAW CENTER, P.C. be retained as the Corporation's legal counsel.

The Chairman stated that the next order of business was to consider the issuance of capital stock of the Corporation pursuant to Section 1244 of the Internal Revenue Code. The Chairman stated that Section 1244 permits ordinary loss treatment, as opposed to capital loss treatment when the holder of Section 1244 stock either sells or exchanges such stock at a loss or when such stock becomes worthless. After discussion, upon motion duly made, seconded, and unanimously carried, it was.

> **RESOLVED,** that the capital stock of the Corporation shall be issued pursuant to Section 1244 of the Internal Revenue Code. The Corporation is authorized to offer and issue its authorized common stock. Said stock shall be issued only for money and other property (other than stock or securities). The officers of the Corporation are authorized and empowered, and directed to perform any and all acts necessary to carry out this plan and to qualify the stock offered and issued under it as Section 1244 stock as that term is defined in Section 1244 of the Internal Revenue Code and the Regulations thereunder.

The Chairman stated that the next order of business was to consider the issuance of shares of the capital stock of the Corporation. The Chairman stated that the following individuals offered to acquire a total of ________ shares of common stock of the Corporation, $__________par value, in exchange for a total of $_______________.

| Name | No. of Shares |
| --- | --- |
| Jack Smith | __________ |
| Jill Jones | __________ |

The Chairman further explained that the stock, upon issuance, is to be fully paid and non-assessable. After discussion, upon motion duly made, seconded, and unanimously carried, it was:

> **RESOLVED,** that in consideration for the payment of ___________Dollars ($______), the Corporation shall issue to Jack Smith shares of the Corporation's fully paid, non-assessable common stock having $____________par value per share.

> **RESOLVED,** that in consideration for the payment of ___________Dollars ($______), the Corporation shall issue to Jill Jones shares of the Corporation's fully paid, non-assessable common stock having $____________par value per share.

The Chairman stated that the next order of business was to consider paying all expenses and reimbursing all persons for expenses paid or incurred in connection with the formation and organization of the Corporation. After discussion, upon motion duly made, seconded, and unanimously carried, it was:

> **RESOLVED,** that the Treasurer of the Corporation be authorized and directed to pay all charges and expenses incident to the formation and organization of this Corporation and to reimburse all persons who have made any disbursements for such charges and expenses.

The Chairman stated the next order of business was to consider reimbursement to officers and Directors of the Corporation of travel and other expenses which such employees expend on behalf of the Corporation. After discussion and upon motion duly made, seconded, and unanimously carried, it was:

> **RESOLVED,** that the Corporation shall reimburse each officer and Director for any reasonable necessary expenses which they incur in connection with the purposes of the Corporation and in furtherance of its business.

> **RESOLVED FURTHER,** that it shall be the policy of this Corporation to reimburse each officer and Director or to pay directly on behalf of each officer or Director necessary and ordinary out-of-pocket expenses incidental to travel for all business activities of the Corporation requiring travel.

The Chairman stated that the next order of business was to consider an election under Section 248 of the Internal Revenue Code to amortize the organizational expense of the Corporation over a period of sixty (60) months, beginning with the first month of business of the Corporation. The Chairman explained that if the election was not made, the organizational expenses would constitute a nondeductible capital expenditure. After discussion, upon motion duly made, seconded, and unanimously carried, it was:

> **RESOLVED,** that beginning with the month in which the Corporation begins business, the Corporation commence amortizing its organizational expense over a period of sixty (60) months in accordance with Section 248 of the Internal Revenue Code.

The Chairman stated that the next order of business was the designation of a depository for the funds of the Corporation. After discussion, upon motion duly made, seconded, and unanimously carried, it was:

> **RESOLVED,** that ______________________________ is designated as the depository for the general account of the Corporation, and all checks, drafts, and orders on any of the accounts with the depository may be signed by the following: Jack Smith or Jill Jones. The President, Secretary and Treasurer are authorized and directed to execute any documents necessary to open and continue any accounts with the depository.
>
> **FURTHER RESOLVED,** that the Secretary of this Corporation be, and hereby is, instructed to annex a copy of such documents to the minutes of this meeting.
> **RESOLVED FURTHER,** that the President or Secretary of this Corporation be, and they hereby are, authorized and empowered to execute any and all other instruments and certificates, and to do and perform all other acts and things necessary, or by them deemed desirable, to effectuate the purposes of the foregoing resolutions.

The Chairman stated that the next order of business was to consider the adoption of a fiscal year for the Corporation. The Chairman explained that the Corporation could elect to end its fiscal year during any calendar month. Upon motion duly made, seconded and unanimously carried, the following resolution was adopted:

> **RESOLVED,** That any one of the President, Secretary or Treasurer of this Corporation, is hereby authorized to select __________________ fiscal year for the Corporation by filing of a tax return, other appropriate tax form, or by any other proper action.

The Chairman stated that the next order of business was to authorize certain corporate officers to execute and deliver deeds, conveyances, promissory notes, deeds of trust, mortgages and other instruments necessary to accomplish the aims and purposes of this Corporation. After discussion, and upon motion duly made, seconded and unanimously carried, it was:

> **RESOLVED,** that the Officers of the Corporation, and only the Officers of this Corporation, be and they hereby are, authorized and empowered, for and on behalf of this Corporation, and as its corporate act and deed, at any time, or from time to time, to negotiate for and/or to enter into any lease, leases, mortgages, promissory notes, other agreement or other agreements with any party or parties, containing such terms and conditions as said Officers may deem necessary or desirable in order to promote and fully effectuate the conduct, by this Corporation, of its business and/or businesses.

The Chairman stated that the next order of business was to establish a time for the regular meetings of the Board.

**RESOLVED,** that the meetings of the Board of Directors of this Corporation be held at the principal office of the Corporation, or at such other location as a majority of the Board may determine, from time to time, as may be called by the President, and that no further notice of such regular meetings need be given.

There being no further business to come before the meeting, upon motion duly made, seconded, and unanimously carried, the Chairman declared the meeting adjourned.

____________________________________

Jill Jones, Secretary

**APPROVED:**

____________________________________

Jack Smith, Chairman

# Appendix D: Directors and Officers Checklist

**CONSENT TO ACT AS DIRECTOR and**
**CONFLICT OF INTEREST CHECK**

TO: **XYX, Inc.** (the "Company")

AND TO: The Board of Directors Thereof

I HEREBY CONSENT to act as Director of the Company if appointed or elected, and to re-appointment or re-election from time to time unless and until this consent shall be revoked by me in writing, this consent to be effective from the date hereof.

Please answer the following questions. If your answer to any of these questions is "yes", please provide details on a separate sheet.

| | | Yes | No |
|---|---|---|---|
| (a) | I am over the age of 18 years; | ☐ | ☐ |
| (b) | I have not been found incapable of managing my own affairs by reason of mental infirmity; | ☐ | ☐ |
| (c) | I am not an undischarged bankrupt. | ☐ | ☐ |

During the preceding 5 years:

| | | Yes | No |
|---|---|---|---|
| (a) | I have not filed for personal bankruptcy nor has any company I have been associated with as an Officer or Director filed for bankruptcy. | ☐ | ☐ |
| (b) | I have not been convicted of a criminal offense (excluding traffic violations and other minor offenses) nor am I the subject of any such pending action, inside or outside of the United States; | ☐ | ☐ |
| (c) | I have not been nor am subject to any order, judgment or decree (which has not been subsequently reversed, suspended, or Vacated), of any court of competent jurisdiction permanently or temporarily enjoining, barring, suspending or otherwise limiting my involvement in any type of business, securities or banking activities; and | ☐ | ☐ |
| (d) | I have not been found guilty by a court of competent jurisdiction (in a civil action), the Securities and Exchange Commission, any state securities agency or the Commodity Futures Trading Commission to have violated a federal or state securities or commodities law or | | |

regulation (which judgment has not been reversed, suspended or vacated). ☐ ☐

## CONSENT TO ACT AS DIRECTOR
(page 2)

During the preceding 5 years, I have acted as a Director or Officer of the following reporting* and/or non-reporting domestic or foreign entities:

| Company Name | Position(s) Held | Period of Service From: To: | Reporting Y/N |
|---|---|---|---|
| | | | |
| | | | |
| | | | |

*a "reporting" company is a company which files periodic financial and management reports with the Securities & Exchange Commission or other foreign securities regulatory agencies.

During the preceding 5 years, I, (or a company I am associated with) have entered into the following agreements with the Company, whereby I receive a direct or indirect benefit (including employment agreements, stock purchase agreements, incentive stock option agreements, etc.): ______________________________________________
______________________________________________
______________________________________________
______________________

I HEREBY UNDERTAKE to promptly notify the Company in the event of any changes in my status.

DATED at ______________________, the ______ day of ____________________, 20____.

______________________________

(signature)

______________________________ (address)

## CONSENT TO ACT AS DIRECTOR

(page 3)

(If you answered "yes" to any of the questions on page 1 (i.e., undischarged bankruptcies, felony convictions or sanctions by SEC or any state securities authority) please provide details below)

______________________________________________________________________

______________________________________________________________________

______________________________________________________________________

______________________________________________________________________

______________________________________________________________________

______________________________________________________________________

____________________________________

______________________________________________________________________

______________________________________________________________________

______________________________________________________________________

______________________________________________________________________

______________________________________________________________________

______________________________________________________________________

____________________________________

______________________________________________________________________

______________________________________________________________________

______________________________________________________________________

______________________________________________________________________

____________________________________________

# Appendix E: Waiver of Notice and Notice of Special Meeting

**WAIVER OF NOTICE OF SPECIAL MEETING OF THE BOARD OF DIRECTORS OF XYZ, INC.**
a Nevada Corporation

We, the undersigned being all of the Directors of XYZ, INC., a Nevada corporation, hereby agree and consent that a special meeting of the Board of Directors of the Company be held on the date and time and at the place designated hereunder, and do hereby waive all notice whatsoever of such meeting and of any adjournment or adjournments thereof.

We do further agree and consent that any and all lawful business may be transacted at such meeting or at any adjournment or adjournments thereof as may be deemed advisable by the Directors present thereat shall be as valid and legal and of the same force and effect as if such meeting or adjournment meeting were held after notice.

Place of Meeting: ______________________
Date of Meeting: ______________________
Time of Meeting: ______________________
Purpose of Meeting: ______________________
__________________________________________________________
__________________________________________________________

__________________________________________________________
__________________________________________________________
__________________________________________________________

DATED this ____ day of __________________, 20___.

____________________________________
JILL JONES
DIRECTOR

____________________________________
JACK JONES
DIRECTOR

**NOTICE OF SPECIAL MEETING OF**
**STOCKHOLDERS OF XYZ, INC.**
A Nevada Corporation

Stockholders:

A special meeting of the stockholders of XYZ, INC., a Nevada corporation, will be held at __________, ______________, on ________________, _______, 20___, at __:__ a.m./p.m.

The purpose of the meeting will be to discuss: ________________________________________
______________________________________________________________________________
______________________________________________________________________________
_____________________________________________________________

In pursuance of the aforementioned action, the stockholders of the Company will be asked to: ____________
____________________________________________________________________
______________________________________________________________________________
______________________________________________________________________

You are cordially invited to attend the meeting in person and you may also use the attached proxy statement to vote your shares.

Dated: ____________________

XYZ, INC.
A Nevada Corporation

____________________________
JACK JONES
Chairman of the Board of Directors

---

PROXY

The undersigned appoints Jill Smith as his/her agent and proxy and authorizes her to act with respect to all securities of XYZ, INC., a Nevada corporation, standing in the name of ______________________________.

Dated: ___________________

________________________________
By: ____________________________
Shareholder

# Appendix F: Minutes of Shareholders Meeting

**MINUTES OF ANNUAL MEETING OF SHAREHOLDERS**
**OF**
**XYZ, INC.**

The Meeting of Shareholders of the above-captioned Corporation was held upon proper notice on ______________________, 20___, at ______, __:__. The meeting was called to order by the President, heretofore elected by the Board of Directors, and the following Shareholders, being a majority of the Shareholders of the Corporation, were present:

**Jack Smith**
**Jill Jones**

Jill Jones was elected temporary Secretary of the meeting and took Minutes of it for the corporate records.

A discussion was then held regarding the election of the Board of Directors for the coming year. As the current Board had performed well in the previous year and wished to continue, upon motion duly made, seconded and unanimously carried, it was

**RESOLVED**, that the following persons are elected Directors for the forthcoming year:

Jack Smith
Jill Jones

Further discussion was held regarding the services rendered by the previous years' Board of Directors, up to and including today's date. Services had well performed. As a result, upon motion duly made, seconded and unanimously carried, it was

**RESOLVED**, that the shareholders ratify the actions of the Board of Directors for the previous year.

There being no further business to come before the meeting, upon motion duly made, seconded and unanimously carried, it was adjourned.

_________________________________
Secretary

# Appendix G: Minutes of Directors Meetings

**MINUTES OF ANNUAL MEETING OF BOARD OF DIRECTORS OF XYZ, INC.**

The annual meeting of the Board of Directors of XYZ, Inc., a Nevada corporation, was upon proper notice on the ____________________, 20___, immediately following the conclusion of the annual meeting of shareholders of the corporation.

Present in person or telephonically were the following Directors:

Jack Smith
Jill Jones

The president called the meeting to order. The meeting then proceeded to elect Officers to serve until the next annual Directors' meeting. The following nominations were made and seconded:

| NAME | OFFICE |
|---|---|
| Jack Smith | President |
| Jill Jones | Secretary/Treasurer |

There being no further nominations the foregoing persons were unanimously elected to the offices set forth opposite their respective names. Each of the Officers so elected thereupon accepted the office to which he was elected as aforstated.

[Insert any specific corporate issues here.]

A discussion was then had regarding the actions taken in the preceding year on behalf of the company.

After further discussion it was:

> **RESOLVED,** that the actions taken by the Officers in the preceding year on behalf of the company were approved and ratified.

THERE BEING NO FURTHER BUSINESS the meeting was adjourned.

________________________________________

Secretary

# Appendix H: Minutes of Directors Meeting

**WRITTEN CONSENT FOR ACTION**
**BY**
**XYZ, INC.**

The Meeting of Shareholders of the above-captioned Corporation was held upon proper notice on ____________, 20___, at ____________, __:__. The meeting was called to order by the President, heretofore elected by the Board of Directors, and the following Shareholders, being a majority of the Shareholders of the Corporation, were present:

Jack Smith
Jill Jones

Jill Jones was elected temporary Secretary of the meeting and took Minutes of it for the corporate records.

A discussion was then held regarding the election of the Board of Directors for the coming year. As the current Board had performed well in the previous year and wished to continue, upon motion duly made, seconded and unanimously carried, it was

RESOLVED, that the following persons are elected Directors for the forthcoming year:

Further discussion was held regarding the services rendered by the previous years' Board of Directors, up to and including today's date. Services had been well performed. As a result, upon motion duly made, seconded and unanimously carried, it was

RESOLVED, that the Shareholders ratify the actions of the Board of Directors for the previous year.

There being no further business to come before the meeting, upon motion duly made, seconded and unanimously carried, it was adjourned.

______________________________
Secretary